The
GEORGIAN
TOWN HOUSE

The GEORGIAN TOWN HOUSE

PAT DARGAN

AMBERLEY

ACKNOWLEDGEMENTS

Permission to include interior photographs from the following is gratefully acknowledged: The Architectural Archive, Dublin; Bath Preservation Trust, Daughters of Charity, Dublin; Dublin Civic Trust; Georgian House and Garden Museum, Limerick; Number Twenty Nine and the National Museum, Dublin; Reddy Charlton; Royal Society of Antiquaries of Ireland. Copyright of the interior photographs of No. 1 Royal Crescent Museum Bath is held by Bath Preservation Trust.

First published 2013

Amberley Publishing
The Hill, Stroud,
Gloucestershire, GL5 4EP

www.amberley-books.com

ISBN 978-1-4456-1403-8 (hardback)
ISBN 978-1-4456-1417-5 (ebook)

British Library Cataloguing in Publication Data.
A catalogue record for this book is available from the British Library.

Typesetting and Origination by Amberley Publishing.
Printed in Great Britain.

CONTENTS

GLOSSARY OF TERMS

Arch	A semicircular or curved head that spans a doorway or window.
Area	The small basement-level yard at the front of a house.
Architrave	The decorated frame around a doorway or window opening.
Ashlar	Regular cut stonework with fine joints.
Balustrade	The protective handrail and uprights of a staircase.
Basement	The floor of a building that lies below the ground level.
Bays	The divisions of an elevation by regular spaces such as windows or columns.
Bonding	The pattern produced on the face of a wall by the method of laying the bricks.
Cantilevered	A staircase built into and supported by a wall.
Capital	The decorated top of a column.
Casement window	Side-opening window.
Chimney breast	The projected body of wall into which the fireplace is set.
Classical	The style of ancient Greek or Roman architecture.
Column	A circular or rectangular pillar.
Corinthian	Renaissance capital with floral and volute arrangement.
Cornice	The decorated moulding positioned at the junction of a wall and ceiling.
Dado	The wooden panel that forms the lower part of an internal wall.
Dado rail	The rail between the dado and the upper section of a wall.
Dentals	A moulding in the form of small projecting squares.
Doorcase	The main entrance to a Georgian house including the door, the surround and the fanlight.
Doric column	Renaissance capital with a square plate and moulded capital.
Dormer	The vertical window built into the slope of a roof.
Eaves	The projecting face at the bottom of a roof where it oversails the wall.

Elevation	The facade of the front, back and sides of a building.
Entablature	The beam or lintel that stretches across the top of a sequence of classical columns.
Fanlight	A semicircular or oval window over a door.
Frieze	A decorated band along the wall immediately below the cornice.
Glazing bar	The light wooden frame that supports the glass and divides a window sash into individual panes.
House block	A group of terraced houses taken together.
Ionic capital	Renaissance capital with a double scroll arrangement.
Jamb	The flat inner edge of a door or window opening.
Keystone	The topmost stone or brick of an arch.
Lintel	The flat beam over a window or door.
Orders	The classification of Classical columns into distinct decorated styles: Doric, Ionic and Corinthian.
Moulding	A narrow, decorated strip of wood or stone.
Palace-fronted block	A block of terraced houses built to appear as a single palace-like building.
Palladian	A style of architecture based on the principles of Andrea Palladio.
Parapet	A low, protective wall built along the edge of a roof.
Pediment	The triangular gable placed over a portico, doorway or window.
Piano nobile	The main floor of a Georgian house, usually at first-floor level.
Pilaster	A shallow column projecting from the face of a wall.
Pitch	The angle of the slope of a roof.
Portico	An open porch marked by a system of columns that support the roof and pediment.
Quoin	The cornerstones of a building.
Render	The thin skin of plasterwork on an external wall.
Renaissance	Historical and artistic period approximately between the fourteenth and seventeenth centuries.
Rustication	The emphasised horizontal and vertical lines of masonry joints in a wall.
Sash	The opening part of a window.
Skirting board	The decorated wooden strip at the base of an internal wall.
String	The side panels of a staircase.
String course	A projecting horizontal band built into a wall.

Stucco	External rendering.
Swag	A plaster decoration in the shape of an extended piece of cloth.
Terrace	A row of houses linked together.
Vault	The underside of an arched brick or stone structure.

THE GEORGIAN IDEAL

Most cities and towns in the British Isles entered a dramatic period of urban remodelling and expansion during the eighteenth century, as tall, slim red brick and stone houses made their appearance in streets and landscaped open spaces. This was the Georgian terraced house building movement and this book, for the general reader, introduces the history, form and character of these Georgian houses. It outlines the origins of the movement and the stylistic influences that impacted on it, charts the building methods used in the construction of the houses, and the explores the spatial qualities that were achieved. In short, it focuses on what makes the Georgian terraced house so elegant and so special. Before looking at these points, it is worth noting that that the term 'Georgian' is a general one and refers to the historic period in British history that corresponds approximately to the reign of the Georgian monarchs, that is, roughly between 1700 and 1830. Before exploring the Georgian town house movement in detail, therefore, it is necessary to step back a little in time to sixteenth-century London, when the forces that prompted and underpinned the movement first emerged.

In 1630, the Earl of Bedford decided to develop his lands at Covent Garden in West London. The earl's house lay along the Strand, and he proposed to develop the open fields at the rear of his mansion for housing. He secured permission to do so from King Charles, but on the condition that the design of the houses be entrusted to the king's architect, Inigo Jones. Jones had visited Italy on a number of occasions where he became acquainted with the development of Renaissance architecture, particularly the works of the Italian architect Andrea Palladio.

During the Renaissance period, the Classical temple front was commonly used as the main element in the elevation of important buildings. This was in essence a large open porch, or portico, with four main elements: a base, a line of tall, circular columns, an entablature, and a pediment. A raised platform was reached by a series of steps which acted as the base, on top of which tall, circular stone columns stretched upwards to the underside of a horizontal beam, or 'entablature', on top of which was a large triangular panel or pediment. The Italian Renaissance architects used the portico as a projecting entrance porch to their building, although the triangular pediment was occasionally omitted. Occasionally, the portico took the form of an applied decorative panel, such as in Edinburgh and Bath, where it acts as the principal element of the elevation of a number of houses.

It is the column tops, or 'capitals', of the columns that classify the Renaissance portico into three 'orders', the origins of which can be traced to the architecture of ancient Greece and Rome. These were the Doric, Ionic and Corinthian orders: all of which, as will later be seen, commonly appear in the capitals of doorcases. The former had the simplest capital and consisted of a shallow mounding with an overhead square plate. The Ionic capital was more complex and had a double scroll with the end spirals, the volutes, facing outwards. More complex again, the Corinthian capital was made up of an arrangement of spirals and stylistic floral patterns.

Jones brought these Renaissance ideas to England in the early seventeenth century when he incorporated them into the design of the Queen's House in Greenwich and King Charles's new banqueting hall in Whitehall. Later, he drew on them again when he laid out the Covent Garden houses for Lord Bedford in the 1630s. Firstly, Jones grouped the Covent Garden houses into a series of terraced blocks, which he arranged around a central open square or piazza. The idea of the terraced houses was not new. It had been in common use in London since the middle ages, as it allowed the builder to squeeze the maximum number of houses into the minimum road frontage. It also helped reduce the construction costs through the use of shared-party walls between the individual houses.

Secondly, Jones's treatment of the elevation of the houses was revolutionary, as he drew heavily on the temple-front ideals of Renaissance Italy. Instead of each house having an individual elevation, Jones laid out each block in the form of a single building. In other words, each block was given the appearance of an Italian Renaissance palace, rather than as a row of individual houses. The ground level acted as a base and consisted of an open arched arcade, with rusticated masonry. That is, the vertical and horizontal joint lines of the masonry were exaggerated. Above this, the second and third floors were divided into bays by a series of Classical columns, or pilasters, which were partially set into the stone walling and stretched upwards to the roof line. A single rectangular window was placed between each column at the first- and second-floor levels, with those on the first floor being noticeably taller. In addition, Jones highlighted the first-floor windows by placing a small triangular pediment over each window head. Jones did not make use of the characteristic triangular portico on top of the columns, but settled for a decorated cornice that stretched just below the roof line and acted as an entablature. Above this, the attic floor was provided with dormer windows set into the roof. In effect, Jones's emphasis was on the total effect, rather than the individual houses. As far as a potential occupier was concerned, it was far more prestigious to live in a 'palace' than a terraced house.

Today, nothing remains of Jones's original houses. The blocks that still exist were built in the nineteenth century and bear only a superficial resemblance to Jones's original design. The Renaissance concepts were repeated, but the scale and massing is different. A number of eighteenth-century drawings, however, show how Jones's design must have appeared, with the rusticated arched base, the upper-floor columns, and the attic storey. The internal layout provided by Jones is uncertain. It is known that the houses were entered from the arcade, above which the first and second floors contained the living accommodation, with the bedrooms on the upper floors.

Some idea of Jones's Renaissance architectural skill can, however, be noted in Lindsey House in the nearby Lincoln's Inn Fields, which dates from 1640, and has been attributed to him. Here, the ground-level arcade used in Covent Garden was filled in, and the arches were replaced with a sequence of windows set into the rusticated masonry. Above this, the two upper storeys were divided into bays by Doric columns, with a single window placed between each column at each level, in an arrangement similar to the Covent Garden houses. Higher up, the decorated balustrade acts as a parapet, behind which the roof seems to have been modified. At a later period the house was remodelled as two independent houses. Fortunately, the only disruption to the house front was the replacement of the original entrance doorway by a pair of independent doors.

Following the emergence of the Covent Garden development, a number of the adjoining landowners, such as the Earl of Southampton and the Earl of St Albans, sought to develop their lands in a similar way. There was, however, a legal difficulty that tended to slow up the entire process, as the selling off of parts of a family estate required the passing of legislation – a time-consuming and expensive process. In 1636 the Earl of Southampton sidestepped this difficulty when he devised a leasing system to simplify his estate development. He marked out the lines of the proposed development on the ground, and then leased out building plots to builders by means of a building lease. Southampton received a yearly rent from the leaseholder and he retained control of the house design through the terms of the lease.

The Southampton leasehold system greatly facilitated the development process and it was soon taken up and used by other developing landowners and builders. The system allowed both the landowner and the builder to make a profit on development ventures, although it was more advantageous to the landowner. He risked little, as his investment was small. He rarely became involved in the building process and his only outlay was for the construction of roads and services. He collected yearly rents over the period of the lease and on the expiry the entire property reverted back to his ownership. The builder on the other hand risked all. He paid for the construction of the house and he had to wait until he successfully leased on the house before he realised his profit. In essence, the Renaissance architecture of Inigo Jones and the leasehold system of Lord Southampton became the model on which all subsequent Georgian town house developments were based for the next century and a half or so, while the motivating factors that lay at the heart of this movement remained profit and style. That is, profit for the landowner and builder; and style in the form of the Renaissance architecture. In this way, the formative seventeenth-century elements of the standard Georgian town were laid in place, from where it progressed to its final form in the following century.

The English architect Inigo Jones visited Italy during the early seventeenth century and brought back, and introduced, the ideals of the Italian Renaissance architecture and town planning into Britain for the first time.

Opposite: A Renaissance-style stone house in Bath. (© Jonathan Reeve)

The incorporation of the Renaissance-style portico – with its base, columns, entablature, and pediment, into building facades – became a characteristic feature of Georgian architecture all over the British Isles.

Above: The decorated capital at the top of the Renaissance column gives the names to the different styles of columns. The Doric capital, with its plain moulding beneath a square plate, is the most elementary of Renaissance capitals.

Above right: The Ionic capital is more complex than the Doric and is characterised by a double scroll, or volute, with the end spirals facing outwards.

Right: The Corinthian capital is by far the most elaborate of the Renaissance capitals. It has a complex stylistic floral arrangement spread beneath a pair of small volutes.

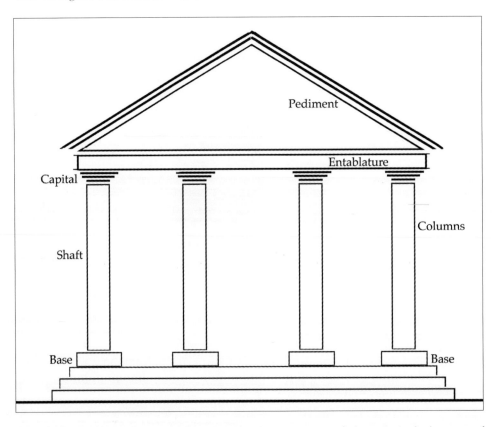

The Roman and Greek temple front, or portico, was one of the principal elements of Renaissance facade. The outline sketch highlights the main components of the portico including the stepped base, tall columns, the crosspiece or entablature, and triangular pediment. It also indicates the division of the Classical columns into the base, shaft and capital.

Left: When Inigo Jones laid out the houses in Covent Garden in London in 1630, he based his design on the Renaissance ideals of the Italian architect Andre Palladio. The cut stone houses were arranged in blocks around the square in the manner of an Italian Palace. The eighteenth-century drawing of the square shows the houses with an open arcade at ground level and double-storey Renaissance columns overhead. The vertically proportioned windows are set between the columns, above which is the roof-level cornice and the attic dormer windows.

Lindsey House in Lincoln's Inn Fields in London is one of the earliest examples of Renaissance stone-built houses in Britain. It is reputed to have been designed by Inigo Jones and follows closely the elevation of the Covent Garden houses. The open arcade at Covent Garden was filled in and windows were included at ground level. At some time in the past, the house was remodelled as two separate dwellings and the doorway was replaced by a pair of independent doors.

2

THE GEORGIAN TERRACED HOUSE

As the seventeenth century moved to a close, the new Renaissance-style housing in Covent Garden and Southampton Square drew increasing numbers of residents. Notwithstanding, there was a difficulty, in that the stone construction was expensive and this restricted the marketing of the houses to the more wealthy purchasers. In 1640, the builder Peter Mills set about addressing this difficulty in his development on Great Queen Street. He followed Inigo Jones's Renaissance ideals, but he built his houses on brick instead of stone, and in this way considerably reduced his costs, and made his profit through the successful sale of his houses. Unfortunately, none of the Mills houses survive, although a sketch of 1843 offers a suggestion of how they looked. The ground floor continued to act as the base, above which the Corinthian columns stretched upwards to the underside of the cornice, with the first- and second-floor windows spaced between them. Like Lindsey House, the heights of the windows varied with the floor levels, and above the cornice, the attic storey was provided with dormer windows. The sketch also shows that the vertically proportioned casement windows varied in height and the sashes were divided into panes. The first-floor windows were the tallest, the ground- and second-floor windows were shorter, while the heights of the attic windows were lower still.

Though none of the Mills houses survive, a block of four similar houses survive in Newington Green, London, dating from 1658. These were built with brick and included Renaissance columns and a decorated cornice. The houses have, however, undergone changes over time. The original windows have been replaced and a shop front has been inserted in the end house at ground level, but three of the doorcases and most of the roof cornice survive.

A little later Nicholas Bardon, one of the most prolific London housebuilders, reduced his building costs even further when he reduced the scale of his houses and simplified the brickwork in his development in Essex Street, London. The width of the house was reduced and the accommodation was squeezed into the narrow spaces between the two party walls. Typically the ground floor had one room to the front and one room to the back, with the entrance hall and stairs located to one side. This was repeated on the upper floors, with the stairs tucked into one corner. Bardon continued with the Mills practice of building in brick, but with a major difference. He discarded the Renaissance columns completely, although he continued to position his tall, narrow casement windows one above the other, as if the columns were still in place. The result was a plain brick elevation relieved only by the vertically proportioned windows, the ground-level doorcase and the overhead cornice.

Surviving examples of these early Bardon-type houses are not common, but notable examples can be seen in Bristol, although these have suffered alterations, particularly by the replacement of the casement windows with vertical sliding sashes. The house in Queen Square, for example, stands three storeys high, with the hooded doorcase to one side. The vertically proportioned windows vary in height, and the floor levels are suggested by a narrow band, or 'string course', while the corners of the house are emphasised by exaggerated cornerstones or quoins. The heavy cornice at roof level is a very prominent feature, with the overhead dormer windows set into the tiled roof. Similarly, the three-storey house in nearby Queen Charlotte Street has tall windows, a pronounced cornice and dormer windows. These types of early houses, with their characteristic quoins, cornices, and dormer windows are often referred to as being in Queen Anne style.

The Building Acts

It was, however, the three London Building Acts that standardised and codified the Georgian terraced town house. The first of these Acts date from 1707 and was introduced as a fire-prevention measure. The Act stipulated that 'party' walls – that is the dividing walls between terraced houses – be raised above the roof, and that wooden cornices at eaves level be replaced by brick parapets. Later, further fire prevention measures, relating to the windows, were introduced under the 1709 Act. By this time the casement windows of Jones and Mills, with their outward opening sashes, had largely been replaced by up-and-down sliding sashes. This change seems to have come about in the early years of the eighteenth century; although it is uncertain whether this was an English or Dutch innovation. The up-and-down sliding movement of the sashes was controlled by balanced weights that were housed in heavy box frames at the sides of the window, and the entire window was positioned flush with the outside of the brick walls. This gave the window frames a very solid-looking appearance. The 1709 Act required that the window be moved back 4 inches from the outer face of the wall, exposing the brick edges around the jambs and window head. This movement of the window back from the outer wall face emphasised the chequer-like arrangement of the elevation, and reduced the danger of fire spreading from window to window.

The Standard Georgian Terraced House

By mid-century the Georgian terraced house building movement had spread all across the land, and Georgian housing developments were carried out in Bath, Bristol, Birmingham, Chester, Dublin and other centres. It was the impact of the 1774 Building Act that finally standardised both the form and construction of the Georgian town house. It introduced further fire-prevention requirements, imposed mandatory building practices and classified the houses into specific 'rates'. The sash box frames were now to be set into chases in the wall so that only a slim section of the box was visible from the outside – thereby further reducing the exposed area of wood and the possibility of fire spread. The Act also set out requirements for the thickness of both the external and party walls in relation to their height. In addition, the Act classified terraced house into four 'rates'. The rates were determined by the floor area, the number of storeys, and height above ground level. For example, the first-rate house was the most impressive. Its large size and width was usually expressed by four or more windows, or 'bays', that stretched across the front. The second-rate house was narrower and was made up of three bays, while the third-rate houses were smaller still and might be reduced to two bays wide. The fourth-rate house was given the smallest floor area. It was usually only two storeys high; but could, nevertheless, be equipped with the characteristic tall sliding windows and an elaborate doorcase.

By this stage, the internal arrangement of the single rooms to the front and back had been established. The number of floors had increased to four and a basement was added. In the case of the elevation, the vertical columns were totally discarded on the grounds of cost, although the Renaissance shadow survived in the vertical proportions of the windows, which continued to be positioned as if the columns remained in place. In effect, the external walls of the houses were now reduced to a chequer of brick panels and window openings. The characteristics of the standard Georgian terraced house were now manifestly complete. One of the characteristics of these town houses is that they are set out with similar elevations and linked together to form unified terraces or blocks. The reason for this, apart from the economic benefit to the landowner and builder, was to conform to the accepted tastes in eighteenth-century street architecture. This frowned on displays of individuality, and required that all houses in a street, or square, should harmonise and merge together. The terraced houses continued to be slotted into uniform blocks, but rarely, as in the case of Bedford Square in London and Queen's Square in Bath, was the full principle of the palace-fronted house attempted. The significance of all this is that Georgian terraced houses are best seen, not so much as individual buildings, but as a street-related, integrated and unified image.

Notwithstanding this, there were a number of instances where the ground-floor levels of some houses were modified and converted to retail use, particularly in the post-Georgian period. In these cases, such as in New Quebec Street in London, and all across the British Isles, the open areas at ground level were paved over and the window openings widened. The enlarged openings were then framed with wooden shop fronts that incorporated an entrance door and overhead facia, while at the same time the original doorways were left in place to provide access to the upper floors which, initially at any rate, remained in residential use.

In essence, the eighteenth-century towns and cities of the British Isles underwent a scale of development never before experienced, as older houses were demolished, new streets and squares were laid out and blocks of elegant Georgian terraced houses were completed. Across the country, landowners, speculators, builders, craftsmen, and investors all involved themselves in the mania of the new house building – the detailed technical mechanics of which will be explored next.

Left: In 1660 Peter Mills built some Renaissance-style houses in Great Queen Street, London. Mills discarded the stone elevations and replaced them with brickwork, while at the same time retaining the double-storey Renaissance columns, the tall windows, the roof-level cornice, and the dormer windows. None of these houses survive, but the nineteenth-century sketch shows the Renaissance elevation executed in brickwork.

Left: The block of four terraced houses in Newington Green in London date from 1658 and, similar to the brick-fronted houses in Queen Street, have their Renaissance elevations built in brick. These include the double-storey columns, vertically proportioned windows and roof-level cornice. The houses have experienced changes over time, but three of the doorcases, the columns, the window openings, and most of the roof cornice survives.

Opposite: Renaissance elements introduced by Inigo Jones were successfully incorporated into the stone elevations of houses in Edinburgh and Bath.

Above left: By the close of the seventeenth century a number of house builders such as Nicholas Barden in London reduced their construction costs by eliminating the Renaissance columns from the brick house fronts, while at the same time retaining the decorative roof line cornice. As a consequence, these houses, for example in Queen Square in Bristol, have a flat brick skin modulated only by the vertically proportioned windows that are positioned as if the columns remained in place.

Above right: The houses in Queen Charlotte Street in Bristol have all the elements of a late seventeenth-century house, frequently referred to as 'Queen Anne' in style. At this period the house fronts followed more Dutch than Palladian ideals. These include plain brick elevation, the decorated wooden cornice, vertically proportioned windows and small attic windows, as well as stone corner, or quoin, stones. Another common feature of the period is the semicircular scalloped head over the entrance door.

Above left: The characteristic decorated roof-level cornice of the late seventeenth-century houses consisted of a gutter and wooden fascia, as well as decorated brackets that projected well out from the face of the wall. The wooden cornices of the houses in Kensington Square in London offer an excellent example of this early feature.

Above right: Following the introduction of the 1707 Building Act, the wooden roof cornice was regarded as a fire hazard and its use was forbidden. It was replaced by continuing the line of the front wall upwards over the line of the gutter to form a brick parapet. This reduced the fire hazard, but partially shielded the view of the roof from the street.

Below: The 1658 date stone on the houses in Newington Green, London was built high up in brick walling. This identifies them as the oldest surviving brick-built Renaissance terraced houses in Britain.

Clockwise from top left: Prior to the eighteenth century, casement house windows that opened outwards were the norm, although few, if any, of these survive today. Sometime during the early part of the eighteenth century the vertical sliding window was introduced and almost immediately replaced the casement type. The up-and-down mechanism was controlled by weights that allowed the opening sashes to slide up and down. These weights were housed in weight boxes that were located on each side of the window. Initially the window, including the weight boxes, was fixed to the sides of the brick opening so that they lined up with the outer face of the brickwork.

The initial positioning of the windows was regarded as a fire hazard and under the 1709 London Building Act the windows were required to be set back 4 inches from the outer face of the wall. This reduced the danger of fire spread and the recessed window introduced an element of depth to the overall elevation.

The 1774 London Building Act sought to further improve fire safety when it required that the window weight boxes be set into chases in the brickwork of the window jamb. The consequence is that only a narrow section of the window frame is visible from the outside – effectively producing a slimmer-looking window.

The development of the standard Georgian terraced house finally emerged following the introduction of the 1774 Building Act. This classified houses into four 'rates'. The first-rate house was the most elaborate. It was given the widest width across the front and had the greatest floor area. One of the main visual characteristics of these large houses is the four or more windows that stretch across the house front, at the first- and upper-floor levels.

The second-rate house was smaller than the first-rate example. It was one of the most commonly built houses and can usually be identified by the three windows that stretch across the front elevation at the first and upper floors.

Third-rate houses were among the most popular forms of the Georgian terraced house, particularly in the regional centres. They had a narrow front that was characterised by a pair of windows at the first and upper levels.

Above left: The fourth-rate house was the smallest of the 1774 rates. It was usually narrow and might reach only two storeys in height. Notwithstanding, it could include all the elements of the standard Georgian House: the brick front, the parapet, the vertically proportioned windows and doors.

Above right: In a number of cases, standard terrace houses were converted to retail at ground level. The open area of the basement was paved over and shop fronts were inserted. At the same time, the original doorway was retained to provide access to the overhead floors, which remained in residential use.

3

FORM AND CONSTRUCTION

Before the standard Georgian terraced house was ready for its first occupants, it went through a long chain of complex legal and on-site operations. First the site had to be secured. Then the main structure of the house had to be built and finally the fitting out of the house interior had to be completed. In most cases the building site was acquired through the Southampton system, where the usual practice involved the landowner leasing off the development land, or a section of it, to a speculator. The speculator then appointed a surveyor who designed and laid out the roads and building plots. Alternatively, the master plan may already have been completed by the landowner. Whichever way, the speculator leased off the building plots, generally in small or single lots. This process was seldom straightforward, as some individuals acted as both speculator and surveyor, while in other cases the surveyor and builder was the same person. In many instances, the leases may have passed through several hands before ending up with the individual willing and experienced enough to build the house. This may have been an investor who wished to hire a builder to construct the house, or it may have been a builder acting on his own behalf. In any event, the goal was to lease the completed house to a tenant as an investment. When taking out the lease, the builder paid a minimum, or peppercorn, rent for the first year. This was an initial token payment to the landowner and it allowed the builder a year in which to build the house and find a tenant, before the first cash payment became due under the lease. All in all, the development process could be a complex affair, with a pattern of leases and several sub-leases, which not infrequently ended up in a tangle of legal disputes.

The Builder
The eighteenth-century house builder was usually a single individual, with a background in construction, such as masonry or carpentry. He rarely carried out the work himself, but hired other craftsmen such as bricklayers, carpenters, or plasterers to carry out and complete the building operation. These workers could be paid in cash, or they could barter their labour in return for building materials which they could then use in building their own Georgian house.

In the initial stage, only the main structure, or shell, of the house was completed, particularly if the work was being undertaken for an investor. That is the walls, the floors, the roof, and possibly the doorcase, windows and stairs were completed – depending on the contract. The reason for this was that the investor, or the owner, was responsible for completing the interior. Where the builder himself was the final owner, or where there was a full building contract, the house was fully completed.

Structure

Before looking at these building operations, it is worth reviewing the overall form of the site and house. The house was set back from the line of the footpath by the front basement area, while stretching behind the house was the long, narrow garden. At the end of the garden was a stable block, which opened onto a back service lane, nowadays referred to as a mew lane. One aspect of the standard terraced house that can be confusing is the relationship between the road level, the ground-floor level and the garden level. The visitor can enter the ground-floor level of the house from the footpath, but on descending the stairs to the basement level and moving into the garden through back door, the visitor will have returned to ground level. The reason for this anomaly lies in the way the house was built.

The basement was the first stage of the house to be completed and it was built at the natural ground level. The roadway in the front was then gradually built up so that the surface and footpath levels ended up just below the ground-floor level of the house. The rear garden represents the original ground, but because of the building up of the street level, it has to be accessed from the basement floor. The logic behind this arrangement was that during the eighteenth century, it was more economic to raise the level of the road than to excavate for the basement.

When laying out the basement accommodation, an open, stone-paved 'area' was left immediately at the front of the house. This allowed an open space onto which the basement door and windows opened. At the ground-floor level, access to the main door was then provided by a short bridge that spanned over this open area. In many cases, the underside of the bridge was later enclosed and fitted with a door that acted as a small entrance porch to the basement, or a scullery. On the street level, both the bridge and the area were protected by a cast iron railing.

Access from the footpath to the lower open area was provided by an external stone or cast iron stairway, in addition to which a coal store was built under the footpath. This was roofed with a brick arch, or vaults, over which the footpath paving was laid. Access to the coal store was from the open area and coal was delivered through a circular chute built into the footpath. This was provided with a small, round cast iron cover set into the paving.

Once the walling of the basement was completed, the brickwork was continued upwards to the roof level, following which the roof was completed. Behind the house, the long, narrow garden was laid out. Many eighteenth- and nineteenth-century town maps indicate that the rear gardens of the Georgian houses were laid out in a formal manner, with geometrically arranged lawns and paths. Whether all the gardens were laid out in this fashion is uncertain, as only a few survive in their original form. The garden of Pickford House in Derby and in one house in the Royal Crescent in Bath have been successfully restored, based on information sourced from old records and drawings, as well as archaeological excavations. In Dublin, an 1838 map of the garden of 63 Merrion Square shows a path enclosing a grassed area. This has been verified by archaeological excavation and the garden has now been successfully restored.

The stable block at the bottom of the garden was usually brick-built, and stood two storeys high. The accommodation included a coach house and stable at ground level as well as storage and staff accommodation in the upper floor. Today, few of these mews buildings survive intact, as they have either been demolished and totally replaced or converted to independent dwellings. This is particularly so in the case of the larger centres such as in London and Edinburgh, where many mews lanes are lined with replaced or converted stable buildings. In a most unusual case, the mews building in Fitzwilliam Lane in Dublin survives intact, and is still used for occasional stabling (Fig. 35). Here the stalls, feeders and saddle brackets are in active use, while the overhead first floor offers visitor accommodation.

Building Operation

In operational terms, the construction of the house carcass was divided into a sequence of craft operations. The bricklayer built the walls, the carpenter was responsible for putting in the floors and roof, and the roof tiler completed the roof. The external, main and party walls of the Georgian house were built mostly in brickwork. These included the chimney breasts, the openings for the fireplace, the flues, the chimneys, parapets, and window openings, as well as the arches for the doorcases. The walls themselves gradually reduced in thickness in steps as they rose upwards through the various floor levels.

In the manufacturing process the brick was made from a special type of brick clay. The clay was moulded by hand into a rectangular shape, usually measuring 9 inches long, 4½ inches wide and 3 inches high, with a small indent, or frog, left on top of the brick to hold the mortar. The fresh clay brick was placed in a kiln and baked, and was then ready for use by the bricklayer. Different clays and different kiln times produced different-coloured bricks. For example, London clays produced yellow bricks, Staffordshire produced red bricks and Cambridgeshire produced light-grey bricks. The thickness of the walls varied and was controlled by the brick size. The walls at lower level might be two brick-lengths wide, higher walls might be a brick and a half wide, while the width of the upper-floor walls might be only a single brick-length. The foundations of the walls were often shallow and usually consisted of widening the base of the brickwork in a series of steps.

The quality of the bricks also varied, and they were divided into facing, or 'stock', bricks and common, or 'placing', bricks. The stock bricks were more carefully made and these were used specifically on the external face of the front and rear walls. The cheaper placing bricks, on the other hand, were used in the inner face of the external walls and in the party walls. In many cases the stock bricks acted only as a face, or veneer, to the external walls and were often only occasionally bonded to the inner placing brickwork.

The bricks themselves were laid in lime mortar, which acted as the binding agent in what was called a 'bond'. This was the pattern in which the bricks were placed against one another in each course. A Flemish bond was the most common type of bond used, and this had a sequence of alternative full bricks laid lengthways called 'stretchers' and half bricks called 'headers'. This created a continuous pattern of alternative headers and stretchers in each course. The finishing touch to the brickwork was the pointing. This was the careful application of mortar to the outer face of the joints between the bricks.

There was one further type of brick commonly used during the Georgian period: the 'rubber'. This was a well-made brick, but the soft surface could be shaped by rubbing the face against a hard surface. This was particularly useful when fashioning the wedge-shaped bricks necessary to build the door arches and window heads. The curve of the arch was formed by laying the wedge-shaped bricks in a radial pattern. The wedge-shaped bricks were also used to form the flat tops, or 'lintels', of the windows, where they were used in an upward splayed pattern. Soft bricks were also occasionally used as a form of dressing around the window and door jambs.

Although the street elevations of the Georgian houses all conform to the accepted standards of uniformity and visual harmony, the backs of the houses were another matter. Here the rear elevations were considered to be of much lesser importance and a less formal approach was consequently adopted. The brickwork remained constant, but the irregular shapes and random alignments of windows, coupled with differing projecting annexes, present an antithesis of Georgian uniformity, as for example in the rear elevation of the Royal Crescent in Bath.

Stucco

In many cases, particularly in London, an external skin of stucco was applied to the ground-floor level of the houses, while the brickwork was retained on the upper levels. The stucco was a type of external rendering and it was usually marked with deep horizontal and vertical lines to imitate the joints of rusticated masonry. This attempt to suggest Renaissance principles was extended in a number of cases, such as in Great Cumberland Place in London, when stucco columns were applied to the upper levels of the brickwork. In an area where brick clay was unavailable or too expensive, the entire building was stuccoed, for example in Bristol. In Whitehaven in Cumbria, all of the Georgian houses were built of stone and finished in stucco. The stucco was undecorated, and the architecture relied on the standard window arrangement and the Georgian doorcases. In a most unusual instance, the central houses in each of the Bedford Square blocks were given the full Renaissance treatment in stucco, with a rusticated ground level, Corinthian columns and a triangle pediment at roof level included.

Stonework

In the early part of the eighteenth century, cut and dressed stonework was very expensive and was only used sparingly. For example, a small number of Georgian houses were provided with stone porches, such as in London and Dublin. In most cases, these porches were in effect miniature Renaissance temple fronts, with stepped bases, ordered columns and flat roofs. In some parts of the country suitable stone was available, and it was the building material of choice, particularly in Bath and Edinburgh. In these areas, the stone was carefully cut into geometric blocks, or 'ashlar'. This could be laid with very narrow mortar joints and made an attractive and strong building material.

In Bath, the form and scale of the Georgian houses follow the standard terraced house arrangements, except for the replacement of brick by the particularly attractive local honey-coloured Bath sandstone. Here the bulk of the four-, three- and two-bay uniform houses present a chequer of plain ashlar and vertical windows, with the occasional use of a Renaissance style door and window pediments. In a number of instances, for example Queen Square, the Circus and the Royal Crescent, the full Renaissance palace front appears. In these cases, the rusticated bases, Renaissance columns, decorated cornices, balustrades, and central pediments were executed in Bath stone. The Georgian houses in Edinburgh followed the same pattern as Bath, although they were built from darker sandstone, and the use of the full Renaissance style is more evident. Here, a large number of two-storey houses have rusticated ground levels with an otherwise plain stone upper level. Many of the larger houses have an undecorated ashlar front elevation, but elaborate dormer windows on the attic level. Unusually, a large number of the Edinburgh houses were given the full Renaissance treatment, with rusticated ground levels, full-height Classical columns, elaborate doorcases, vertically proportioned windows, and deep roof-level cornices.

Artificial stone was occasionally used as an alternative to stone, particularly where fine or intricate work was required. This was usually manufactured from clay and sand, which was moulded into panels and baked in a kiln. The most widely used of these was 'Coade' stone, which was manufactured in London and distributed all around the county. The manufacturing plant was operated by Eleanor Coade and produced an extensive range of distinctive designs. The Coade catalogue of 1778 carries illustrations of quoin stones, mouldings and keystones, all of which were common features in Georgian London, for example the surrounds to the doorway in Harley Street and the keystones used in Bedford Square.

Woodwork

As the walling of the house was being constructed, it was necessary to complete the wooden floors at each level as the brickwork progressed. In this way, they provided a working platform as the building height increased, in addition to their primary flooring purpose. Most of the floors in the house consisted of wooden joists that spanned between the brick walls. These were stretched between the brick walls, and were often fitted into sockets left in the brickwork, or rested on steps created when the wall thickness was reduced. Where floor spans were particularly wide, heavy wooden beams were placed between the walls to help carry the joists. The flooring boards were laid at a right angle to the line of the joists, and they were butted tightly together. When the brickwork reached the roof line, the roof was constructed. It was built from wooden rafters, with the twin slopes arranged in the form of an 'A'. In practice, there were three types of roof structure commonly used during the eighteenth century. The first consisted of a simple pitched 'A'-type structure that spanned from front wall to back wall, parallel to the street. A more common type was the double-pitched roof. This consisted of a pair of 'A'-type roofs that stretched across the house. The significance of this was that, in addition to having a low profile, it was shielded by the parapet, and was almost invisible from the street. Another roof type commonly used was the Mansard. Here, the back and front sides were almost vertical, while the top was almost flat. This created an adequate space within the roof structure for the attic rooms.

All the roofs, whatever their type, had to be made waterproof, and this was achieved by the roof covering. In the early years of the eighteenth century, clay tiles were commonly used, but as more slate quarries were opened and the century progressed, the use of slate came to dominate. In both cases, the crown of the roof was sealed by inverted 'V'-shaped clay ridge tiles. Both the tiles and slates were secured to the roof timbers in the same manner. Light wooden rails, or 'battens', were laid across the roof timbers at right angles, and the tiles or slates were nailed to these. In addition, lead sheeting, or 'flashing' was used to form the gutters and seal the joints around the chimneys and parapets.

Windows

Aside from the brickwork, the main characteristic features of the Georgian house are the windows and the doorcases. As a rule, the windows of the Georgian houses were vertically proportioned, that is, with heights that related to the ceiling heights of the rooms they served. As the ceiling heights of the rooms varied, so also did the window heights. The ground- and first-floor windows were the highest, the second-floor windows lower, and the third-floor and basement windows lower still, all echoing the hierarchical nature of the floors they served. Each opening section, or 'sash', was divided into small glazed panes by narrow glazing bars, and the number of panes varied. The tall windows on the first floor usually had fifteen panes, the ground- and second-floor windows had twelve panes, while the smaller windows of the basement and top floors might be reduced six panes. This characteristic feature of multiple glass panes was driven by cost factors, as the small panes of hand-made 'crown' glass of the period were less expensive than larger panes. A projecting stone sill was embedded into the wall immediately below the window. This deflected the rainwater run-off from the window and avoided staining the brickwork immediately underneath.

Variations to the standard window design were not unusual. For example, windows in square openings were divided into three panels by heavy wooden uprights. This gave the window a decided overall vertical proportion. Round-headed windows also made an occasional appearance, particularly in rear elevations. Less common was the distinctive 'Venetian' window. This was made up of a tall central sash with a rounded head, which was flanked on both sides by lower flat-headed sashes.

Bay windows were another occasional feature of the standard house, particularly in London. These projected outwards from the main walls, with splayed sides, and occasionally extended over several floor levels. In more elaborate cases, a bow window was formed. These were generally confined to rear walls where the brick or stone bow-shaped projection extended from the basement level to the top floor, into which a pair of standard windows was set at each floor level. Another frequently used window type was the attic dormer. Here, the vertical face of the sash was built into the slope of the roof, with the side and top sheeted in lead or slate.

Doorcases

Despite the rigid uniformity of the brick fronts, the builders of Georgian houses managed to introduce one element of variety into the facades of the standard houses. This was the entrance doorcase, which in essence consisted of a semicircular or flat-headed opening into which the panelled door and its frame was set, with the door itself equipped with a brass knocker and doorknob and a box lock on the inside. These doorcases are one of the outstanding features of the Georgian house, and they vary considerably in their scale and complexity. The most modest examples had a panelled door set into a plain frame, with an overhead fanlight that allowed natural light to enter the entrance hall. These earlier fanlights were rectangular in shape, with geometric panels set into metal glazing bars. In addition to the fanlight, the early doors were often given overhead projecting canopies, or hoods, supported by projecting brackets. In a number of instances, such as in Bristol, the hoods were semicircular scallop-shaped hoods. The early rectangular fanlights were soon replaced by semicircular examples, which were also given intricate geometric patterns.

The more elaborate doorcases took the form of miniature temple-style Renaissance porticos. Here the door opening was framed with a pair of columns, with a fanlight and pediment overhead. The larger and most important Georgian town houses had the most elaborate doorcases. In these cases the central door was flanked on either side by narrow side lights, with a semicircular fanlight – with the entire doorcase set into the wide round-headed opening. Even more elaborate doorcases, particularly those in the homes of the prosperous, were framed with miniature Renaissance elements such as ordered columns and decorated entablatures, with the addition of wide semicircular overhead fanlights. These miniature temple-style doorcases are particularly common in Dublin, while in a number of London examples, such as in Bedford Square, the doorcase opening is framed with alternative blocks of brick and Coade stone. Another type of doorcase that made an occasional appearance was Gibbs surround. In this case, the door opening was emphasised by the staggered and exaggerated stone or stucco block arrangement around the opening. Taken together, the range of doorcase forms and elements that were available to the Georgian housebuilders allowed for the production of an almost limitless range of door fronts. The doors themselves usually consisted of a configuration of six panels set into the framework, although eight- and nine-panel arrangements were occasionally availed of.

Ironwork

Cast iron was another material commonly used in the construction of the standard Georgian house, in the form of railings, balconies, foot scrapers, lamps, and snuffers. The railings around the open area at the front of the basement and across the connecting bridge served to prevent anyone falling into the basement, as well as being a decorative feature. At their simplest, the railings consisted of a sequence of vertical uprights, spaced along horizontal rails. Most of the railings had plain uprights, but some uprights carried arrow tip heads and other decorative features. Occasionally, the most prestigious houses were given very elaborately decorated rails and corner posts.

A common, but not universal, feature in houses was the addition of balconies to the house fronts, usually at first-floor levels. Only rarely were these balconies in the true sense. Instead, they were simple box frames, or window guards, that were bolted to walls under the windows. Like the railings, some were made up with plain vertical uprights, while others were given highly decorative patterns. The fitting of these balconies became particularly common during the second part of the eighteenth century when factory-made examples could be purchased from manufacturer's catalogues, which offered an extensive range of geometric designs including spirals, grills and floral, many with a Regency flavour.

A common features of the Georgian streets was the high degree of mud and animal droppings that lay around, and in order to prevent this material from being brought into the house by shoes and boots, a low foot scraper was often provided outside the main door. This allowed footwear to be scraped clean before entering the house. They were often small, elegant pieces of eighteenth-century metalwork, with a low horizontal blade set between a pair of supporting legs. In the more elaborate examples, the legs were elaborately decorated and the underside of the blade had a curved outline to help clean the top of the shoes or boots.

External cast iron lamps were another feature of some houses, particularly in Bath, where an impressive range can be found. In the simplest examples, the lamp was supported on an arm that projected out from the front wall of the house near the entrance door. This was often decorated with stylistic floral or other designs. The next type is much more elaborate, with the high-level lamp holder positioned at the crown of the metal arch that spanned the entrance steps of the house. Elsewhere, for example in Edinburgh, the lamps were supported by tall, free-standing metal posts. The lamps were originally oil fired with glass domed covers, although today electricity has replaced the oil system. In addition to the lamp, a snuffer was frequently provided. This was usually mounted on the wall near the outside lamp, and consisted of a hollow cast iron cone into which a taper, or naked flame, could be inserted and quenched.

Services

The sanitary services in the typical Georgian town house were almost non-existent. The water supply, if it existed at all, was gravity fed, and the pressure was consequently low. Where a water supply did exist it was delivered to the basement level where it had to be stored in special cisterns. From here, the water could be circulated around the house by means of a hand pump, or had to be carried in containers to the upper floors of the house by hand. Where no water supply existed, as was often the case, each house had a well in the back garden to cater for the household needs. Some of the houses were equipped with a system of water collection, where rainwater was collected from the roof and stored for use later.

The disposal of household sewage was another difficulty. Most Georgian houses had no drainage system until the middle of the nineteenth century, so waste disposal had to be catered for in the garden. This consisted of a deep hole or 'cess pit' into which the sewage and waste from the house were discharged. The pit was covered by a wooden plank, with a hole through which the sewage was emptied into the pit. When a cess pit was full, it was covered over and a fresh pit excavated in another area of the garden – an operation that might have to be repeated many a time over the lifespan of the house. In some areas a sewage collection system was operated by the 'night soil' collectors. These were individuals who collected the soil and other household waste each night from the back lanes and disposed of it in local markets for fertiliser.

Pattern Books

One of the intriguing aspects of the Georgian town house building movement is the consistent level of architectural and technical skill achieved by the eighteenth-century builders all across the country – an aspect that raises the question as to how the builders received these necessary skills. The architects of the period seem to have played little or no part in the design or construction of the standard terraced houses, except in the case of large individual houses. Instead, the builders were forced to rely on a range of publications called 'pattern books' for information. These were published throughout the eighteenth and nineteenth centuries and included, for example, Peter Nicholson's *The New Practical Builder and Workman's Companion*, Batty Langley's *The Builders Jewel*, and James Gibbs's *Book of Architecture*, all of which offered detailed information and technical illustrations relating to construction technology, as well as guidance on the proper use of Georgian proportion and design principles. The Gibbs 1728 *Book of Architecture* offers numerous designs for windows, fire surrounds and doorcases, while the Nicholson work of 1823 provides clear information and illustrated views of floors, stairs, roofs, windows, as well as structural details for floors and walling. Working from these, the eighteenth-century builders were able to acquire the skills and knowledge necessary to complete their building contracts: whether these were limited to the superstructure or extended to the entire structure.

Originally the open area at basement level was not landscaped. Today it offers great scope for a potted flower garden, which can add to the environment of both the house and the street.

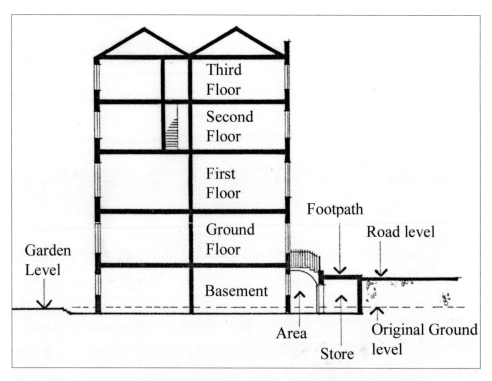

Cross-section through the typical Georgian terraced house. This highlights the relationship between the original ground level, the new road level and the house floor levels.

Access to the front door of the house was provided by a short bridge that spanned across the open area. Today the underside of many of the bridges has been filled in with an entrance porch to the basement, or a scullery.

Above: The open area under the entrance bridge was often filled in with an entrance porch to the basement or a scullery.

Above right: In order to prevent passing pedestrians from falling into the open area it was protected by cast iron railings generally set on stone plinths. Today the railings are painted black, although originally they were mostly painted a bronze colour or green.

Right: Access from the footpath to the lower basement area was provided by a stone or cast iron stairway. This was for the use of the household servants, visiting tradesmen or for the delivery of supplies.

Above: The coal store, which was entered from the basement open area, was located under the footpath. This had a curved, brick-vaulted roof and the coal was delivered through a circular chute that was incorporated into the vault and was accessed from the overhead footpath. A second store under the footpath for other goods might be provided in the wider houses.

Below left: The delivery chute from the coal store opened in the footpath, and was given a circular cast iron cover that was set flush into the footpath. Many of these covers have been removed in the past, but those that survive often have decorated patterns on the face. In these instances they add an extra rhythm to the pattern of the stone paving.

Below right: The cast iron covers of the coal chute could be prone to rainwater penetration where they sat into the stone paving and, in order to minimise this, small drainage channels and runoffs were occasionally cut into the face of the paving stones.

Above: The great majority of the Georgian terraced houses were given gardens at the rear. Unfortunately, many of these have been built over and obliterated. Today a number of gardens in Bath and elsewhere have had their formal paths and landscapes successfully restored.

Below: Mews-type coach houses and stable buildings were a feature at the rear of most Georgian houses and opened onto service lanes. Today most of these buildings, such as in Gloucester Mews in London, have either been replaced or remodelled as independent dwellings.

Above left: A number of mews buildings, for example in Edinburgh, have been sympathetically remodelled with their original structure, brickwork, windows and doors intact.

Above right: The coach house and stable in Fitzwilliam Lane in Dublin is one of the rare examples where, not only has the original mews structure survived intact, but the building remains in active use as a stable.

Below: Internally, the Fitzwilliam Lane coach house and stables in Dublin is still equipped with stalls, hay racks, water troughs and harness brackets. On the upper floor the original staff accommodation remains in residential use.

Bricks were handmade and measured 9 inches long, 4½ inches wide and 3 inches high. Many had a depression, or frog, on the top to hold the mortar. The mortar was made with sand and lime and this allowed the brickwork to breathe. It is vital to remember that when repairing or re-pointing Georgian brickwork, a lime-base mortar is used, as modern cement mortars can damage the bricks. The colour of the brick used varied throughout the British Isles and included plum, red, yellow, or grey – depending on the construction date and the local clay types.

The bricks used in the building of the Georgian house were generally laid in either a Flemish or English bond. The Flemish bond was by far the most common and consisted of laying each line, or course, of bricks in an alternative arrangement, with each long side of the brick followed by the shorter end side, technically referred to as 'header and stretcher'.

Where an arch was used to span a door or window opening, the bricks were laid in a radial fashion. The soft bricks, or rubbers as they were known, were shaped into a wedge by rubbing the sides on a hard surface and these were then laid with the line of the joints radiating from the centre point of the arch.

Where the doors or windows were provided with flat heads the bricks were laid in an upward-splayed fashion. These, like the arch bricks, were also rubbed into the required wedge shape on a hard surface.

In contrast to the formal uniform house fronts, the rear elevations of the Georgian houses could be highly irregular, as can be seen everywhere, particularly in the larger centres, where houses of different sizes and depths and with different rear projections were built side by side – a lack of uniformity not expressed in the street fronts. (*Below:* © Jonathan Reeve)

Above left: A common feature of many standard Georgian houses was the use of a rendered or stucco panel on the external face of the wall, at ground level. This was an attempt to give a Renaissance-style base to the houses. The stucco could be finished either smooth or rusticated. In the case of the rustication, exaggerated lines were inscribed into the plaster to suggest stonework.

Above right: In some instances the entire elevation of the houses was rendered in plain stucco. This is particularly characteristic of some regional areas such as in Whitehaven in Cumbria, where bricks were unavailable or particularly expensive.

Left: In some brick houses, particularly in London, stucco was used to suggest a Renaissance elevation, similar to Lindsey House. Rustication was applied at ground level, above which shallow columns carried up between the windows to the stucco roof cornice.

Right: In a small number of cases, for example in Bedford Square in London, the full Renaissance elevation was created by facing the entire building with stucco. The ground level was rusticated and a shallow temple front, complete with triangular pediment, was applied to the upper floors.

Below left: In an unusual example the rear windows of a house in Bath were formally arranged in clusters of three, on the three floor levels. (© Jonathan Reeve)

Below right: The elevations of the Georgian houses were often enhanced by landscaped settings. (© Jonathan Reeve)

Above left: Small Renaissance open temple-fronted entrance porches were an occasional feature, particularly in London. These projected out from the main wall of the house and could be completed in stone or painted wood. The free-standing columns were often given Doric or other capitals as well as a moulded fascia on the flat roof suggesting an entablature.

Above right: One open-fronted, stone-built, temple-fronted porch in Dublin follows closely the Renaissance ideal. It has a pair of bold Doric columns on the outside, as well as similar but shallower inner columns set into the brickwork. In addition, the line of flat roof was emphasised by an elaborately moulded entablature.

Left: The more elaborate doorcases represent the high point of eighteenth-century craftsmanship, with slim glazing bars, accurate classical decorations and skilfully carved ordered capitals on the columns.

Above left: In Bath, delicate honey-coloured stonework completely replaced brickwork. Here the smaller, modest houses are characterised by plain ashlar elevations. That is, the stonework is accurately cut and squared in geometric blocks and carefully laid with narrow mortar joints. The result is a blend of the vertically emphasised windows and doors set into the plain chequer of Bath stone, contrasted by the black cast iron railings.

Above right: The elevations of the more elaborate houses in Bath are occasionally characterised by projecting porches at ground level. In addition, the main windows are decorated with projecting architraves, hoods and triangular pediments.

Right: The most elaborate of the Bath houses, such as those in the Royal Crescent, were given the full Renaissance treatment. Here the continuous uniform ashlar walls are modulated by bold Ionic columns set into the honey-coloured masonry and topped by a deep, highly decorated roof-level cornice.

The terraced house block in Queen Square in Bath offers an excellent example of the successful application the Renaissance palace-fronted ideal. The three-storey block is rusticated at ground level, with flat, double-height, rectangular Corinthian columns built into the masonry. The block has an impressive central bay with six half-round columns and a large triangular pediment at roof level, in addition to which the impact of the palace front is emphasised by a projected bay with semicircular columns at each end.

In Bath, the Renaissance temple-front element has been successfully given a prominent central position within the wide sweep of Lansdown Crescent. (© Jonathan Reeve)

Above left: Edinburgh is another example where the brickwork has been replaced by stonework: in this case a local sand-coloured stone. Most of the houses extend to three storeys or more with an attic storey over. The majority have rusticated ground levels with plain ashlar masonry overhead. An unusual and interesting feature is the range of often complex dormer windows.

Above right: The Renaissance ideals were introduced to the larger and more important Edinburgh houses. These vary in height between three and four storeys and, in addition to the ground-level rustication, have shallow columns built into walls between the windows.

Right: Edinburgh also has a range of smaller, double-storey houses. Despite their minimal scale they were given rusticated ground levels and in one instance a stone balustrade acts as a parapet.

During the late 1700s a number of artificial stone elements and decorations were produced. The most popular of these was Coade stone, produced by Eleanor Coade in her workshop in London. The range of elements was extensive, as can be seen from the Coade catalogue of 1778 that offered quoin stones, decorated blocks, mouldings, and keystones.

The Coade stone elements were available all over the country, but were most popular in London where, for example, a number of key stones representing a human face crown the arched doorways of the houses in Bedford Square and elsewhere in the city.

Internally the flooring boards of the Georgian houses were much wider than those of the present day. The boards were generally made from Baltic fir or pine, although in the most expensive houses oak could be used. The floor boards butted tightly against one another and, unlike modern flooring, they were not tongued and grooved. The flooring was for the most part left bare, with only the occasional use of decorative rugs, as wall-to-wall carpeting was not a feature of the Georgian period.

The mansard roof was a characteristic feature of many standard Georgian terraced houses. This had very steep sides as well as an almost flat roof, which accommodated an attic storey into the roof space.

Clay roof tiles covered the roofs of most of the Georgian houses in the early part of the eighteenth century. The tiles had a semicircular profile and were fixed to the roof timbers with nails. Like the bricks, they were made from clay and baked in a kiln.

From the middle of the eighteenth century onwards slate took over as a roof covering, as it became more available and offered a more successful method of waterproofing the roof. The slates were laid so that they overlapped one another and were fixed to the roof timbers with nails. At the vulnerable apex of the roof the slating was sealed with 'V'-shaped clay ridge tiles.

Above: The windows of the standard Georgian house varied in height according to the heights of the rooms they served. The vertically sliding up-and-down window sashes were controlled by a system of cords and weights. The sashes themselves were divided into small panes. The Georgian glass was cut from large discs and can often be identified by its slightly irregular surface and colour.

Above right: Occasionally, round-headed windows made an appearance. Here the arrangement of the vertical sashes followed the normal practice, but with a semicircular head on the top sash.

Right: Most windows in the Georgian house had a decidedly vertical proportion. Where this was not so, such as in the case of a square opening, the sashes were arranged in a Venetian form. This had a wide central sash which was flanked by narrower sashes on either side – together creating a decidedly vertical emphasis.

Above: Round-headed windows were generally confined to the ground- or first-floor levels of the Georgian houses, although occasionally the curve-headed windows might feature on a number of levels, such as in Great Percy Street, London.

Left: The Venetian window had a distinctive form, but was used sparingly. Here three narrow sashes were grouped close together. The central sash was the tallest and had a round head, and this was flanked on each side by lower and narrower flat-headed sashes.

Right: Bay windows made only an occasional appearance in Georgian terraced houses, particularly in London. These had a main sash to the front as well as splayed side sashes. Mostly the bay windows were confined to a single level but occasionally, such as in Bryanston Square in London, the bay extended over several levels.

Below: The dormer windows in the attic tended to have small sliding sashes that were fitted vertically into the sloping sides of the roof. The vertical sides and flat roof were sheeted and weathered in lead, slate or tiles, depending on the roof covering.

Opposite: Semicircular bow windows were another element occasionally used, although they were generally confined to the back of the houses. In these cases, the curved brick walling of the bay projects outwards from the main wall of the house, into which standard windows were inserted at the various floor levels.

Top (both): The entrance door was one of the main features of the Georgian house and it was equipped with brass or cast iron door furniture, including a prominent door knocker. In the early days of the Georgian period, the door furniture, such as the knockers, was cast iron, often with human and animal representations, but this soon made way to more sinuous organic brass fittings.

Right: The doorknob, like the knocker, could be brass or cast iron. Letter boxes which often matched the original brass or cast iron furniture were only inserted at a later date.

Opposite top: Inside, the entrance door of the Georgian terraced house was secured by an internal box-type door lock. This was often decorated with brass edges, knobs and detailed trimming.

Opposite bottom: The lock box on the inner face of the entrance door was a significant element, and could be decorated with brass keyholes, a doorknob and ornamental scrolls.

Right: Being the place where both visitors and owners would enter, the design of the entrance was of utmost importance. Even the more modest houses were provided with panelled doors and overhead fanlights.

Below: The fanlight over the entrance doors allowed natural light to entrance hall, which otherwise would be dark. The early fanlights tended to be square or rectangular, where intricate geometric patterns were often formed by the narrow glazing bars.

Left: The early entrance doorways often had projecting hoods. These were usually flat with moulded edges and were supported by decorated brackets that extended out from the walls.

Below left: In the more important houses, the jambs of the door opening had rectangular or semicircular columns. These were extended upwards to support hood brackets. The use of such wooden hoods and brackets was discontinued as a fire prevention measure.

Below: Semicircular hoods were a common feature of early houses. These are decorated on the underside with shell-like scallops, and like the simpler flat hoods are supported by projecting brackets.

Above: Another unusual example in Bristol has a triangular pediment with a broken base line, rectangular columns and capitals as well as foliage-like panes set into a rectangular fanlight.

Below (both): Following the introduction of the London Building Acts, most of the standard Georgian terraced houses were given a simple panelled door with an overhead semicircular fanlight to conform to fire safety standards. This eliminated the woodwork around the door except for the fanlight, where decorative patterns were formed by the glazing bars.

Above left: In the early, more elaborate, doorcases, temple-front elements were sometimes introduced. These could include side columns and capitals as well as pediments – in an unusual early instance in Bristol, the pediment has a curved and broken outline.

Above right: Many Georgian doorcases are characterised by miniature Renaissance temple fronts. A number in Bristol, for example, have half-round Doric columns, a semicircular fanlight with radial glazing bars and a triangular pediment.

Left: In the late Georgian period, naturalistic and organic patterns such as flower petals began to make an appearance in the fanlights over the entrance doors.

Above left: By varying the scale, style and complexity, the Georgian builders could introduce an almost limitless variety of doorcases that fitted well into the uniform streetscape.

Above right: The doorcases in the major Georgian centres tend to be the most elaborate. In one example in London, narrow side lights flank the door and a wide fanlight fills the semicircular arch. This extra glazing allows a plentiful supply of natural light into the hall.

Right: The larger, temple-fronted doorcases usually include Doric or Ionic columns on each side of the door. These are flanked by narrow side lights with quarter columns at the outside edge of the opening, spanned by a decorated entablature or crosspiece. Above this, a wide fanlight completely fills the full width of the arch.

Opposite: Renaissance-style temple fronts are a characteristic feature of the large doorways all across the British Isles, particularly in the case of prosperous households. In these cases the doorcases are set into wide semicircular brick or stone arched openings.

Right: The fanlights of the wider doorcases were usually elaborate with complex arrangements of intricate radial and fanlike patterns formed by the glazing bars. These were wooden or metal and gradually reduced in lightness over the Georgian period.

Below: Some of the more impressive doorcases were very bold indeed. A number in Dublin, for example, have half-round Doric columns, wide side lights and outer rectangular columns. An entablature spans the full width, while overhead the narrow fanlight is framed within a semicircular frieze.

Opposite: Many of the London doorcases were equally bold. A number in Bedford Square and elsewhere have vertical side lights, and a full-width semicircular fanlight, with the arched opening emphasised by alternative blocks of Coade stone and brick.

Above left: The doorway to the Georgian town house took many forms, with the basic idea of establishing an imposing entrance. It commonly had six raised panels set into the side styles and cross rails. The middle cross rail was generally the widest and strongest, into which the door lock and handle were set.

Above right: Where householders wished to make an impression on callers, the number of door panels could be increased to eight. In addition, a vertical chase was cut into the wide central upright, to create the impression of a double door.

Right: The Gibbs type of doorcase is another commonly used doorcase. Here the narrow doorways and the semicircular fanlights are set into a sequence of alternative spaces and blocks. This type was usually made with stucco or, in exceptional cases, stone.

Left: An increase in the number of door panels to nine or even twelve was another gesture undertaken with the hope of creating an impressive entrance to the house.

Below: One of the principal external characteristics of the Georgian terraced house was the cast iron railing that enclosed both the entrance bridge and the basement area. These were generally set into a stone plinth, and the tops of the more modest examples were pointed to resemble spearheads.

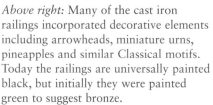

Above right: Many of the cast iron railings incorporated decorative elements including arrowheads, miniature urns, pineapples and similar Classical motifs. Today the railings are universally painted black, but initially they were painted green to suggest bronze.

Above left: Cast iron railings that incorporated elaborate Renaissance-inspired elements such as globes or scrolls signalled the homes of wealthy landowning or merchant families.

Right: In the case of the more imposing houses, decorated corner posts were often incorporated into the cast iron railings. These could be elaborate works of art indeed and could feature column-like posts, organic scrolls and lamp holders.

Left: First-floor cast iron balconies are a feature of many Georgian houses. These are not balconies in the strict sense, but decorative box frames fixed to the walling surrounding the window openings, particularly at first-floor level. The simpler balconies had plain uprights and many are later additions. Today these are often used for the display of flower baskets.

Below: Many of the cast iron balcony designs have elaborate decorative and geometric patterns and were often mass produced, particularly during later periods. They can apply a unifying influence to a terraced block.

Opposite: In an unusual example in Amwell Street in London, the first-floor windows and the highly ornate balconies were set into semicircular brick arches.

As a precaution against bringing muddy or dirty footwear into the house a cast iron doorscraper was provided outside the entrance door. This allowed boots and shoes to be scraped clean before entry to the house. At its simplest, the scraper consisted of a narrow blade set between a pair of short legs.

The more elaborate doorscrapers were provided with decorated legs and a double-edged blade. The sole of the boot or shoe could be scraped along the flat top of the blade, while curved bottom allowed the top of the boots to be cleaned.

Despite its small size, the cast iron boot scraper in the larger houses could be impressive, with its highly stylistic foliage decoration.

Above: There was no street lighting in Georgian times and many house fronts had external lamps. These were oil operated, and were held in decorated cast iron brackets that projected out from the wall. A number of brackets in Bath, for instance, have a delicate interwoven floral design.

Right: Lansdown Crescent in Bath has a particularly impressive range of lamp holders. These consist of ornate and delicate cast iron arches that span the entrance to the house bridges, with the lamps positioned high up on the crest of the arch.

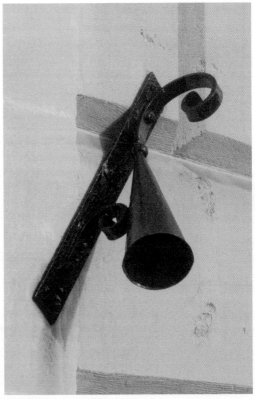

Above left: Duncan Terrace in Islington has one of the few London examples where arched lamp holders survive. The lamp itself no longer exists, but the plain arched upright and lamp holder survives.

Above right: The external house lamps were lit by candles or tapers when required. Afterwards the tapers or candles were extinguished by inserting them into hollow, cast iron, cone-shaped snuffers fixed to the wall.

Left: Edinburgh has a range of arched and upright lamp holders. The tall, simple upright holders are positioned near the doorways, with the high-level lamps suspended from delicate curved brackets.

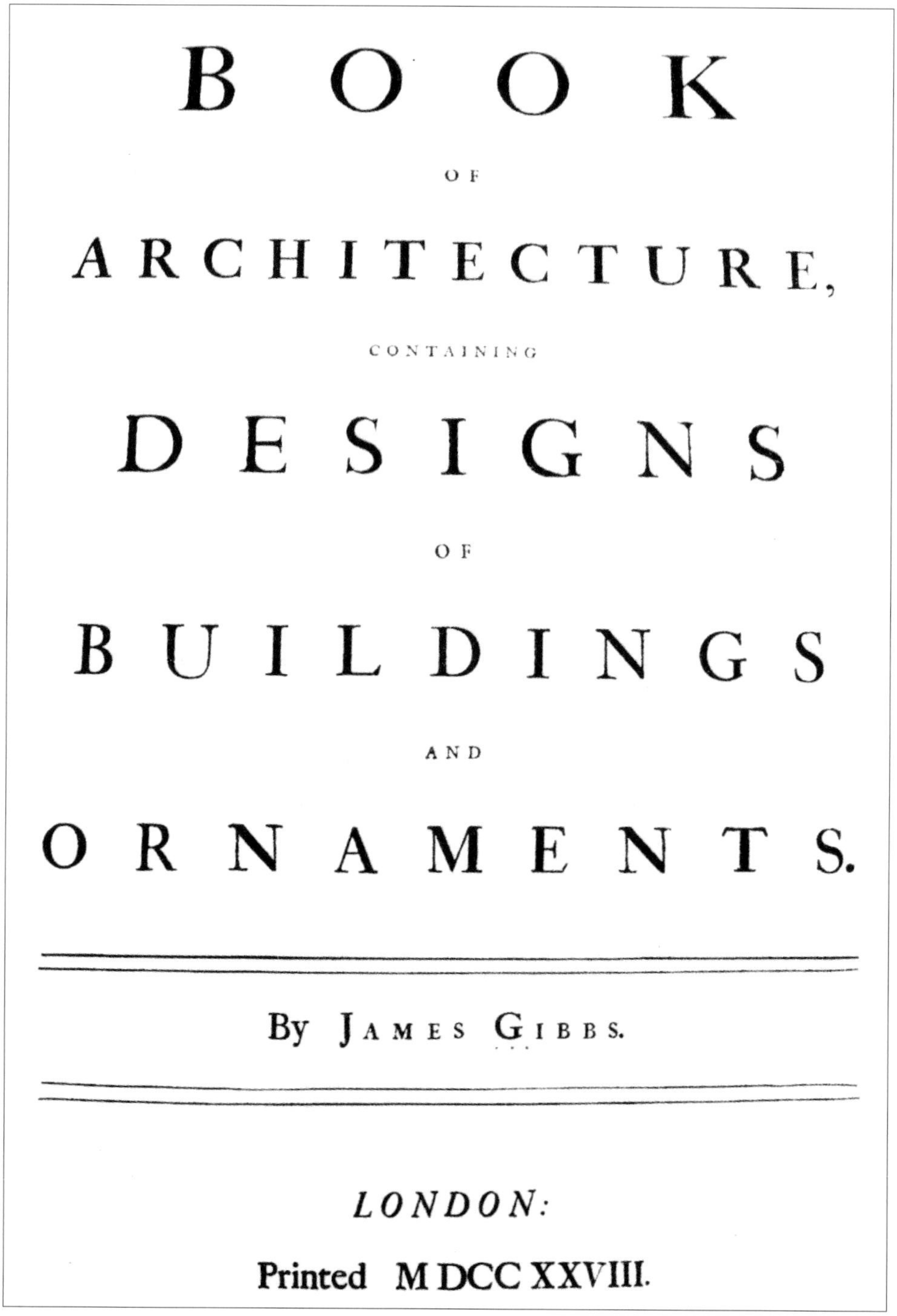

B O O K

O F

ARCHITECTURE,

CONTAINING

D E S I G N S

O F

B U I L D I N G S

A N D

O R N A M E N T S.

By JAMES GIBBS.

LONDON:

Printed MDCCXXVIII.

Georgian house builders acquired their construction information from pattern books such as the 1728 James Gibbs *Book of Architecture Containing Designs of Buildings and Ornaments.*

Plate from James Gibbs's *Book of Architecture, Containing Designs of Buildings and Ornaments*, of 1728. This offers a design for a Gibbs-type doorcase. These books provided technical and architectural information.

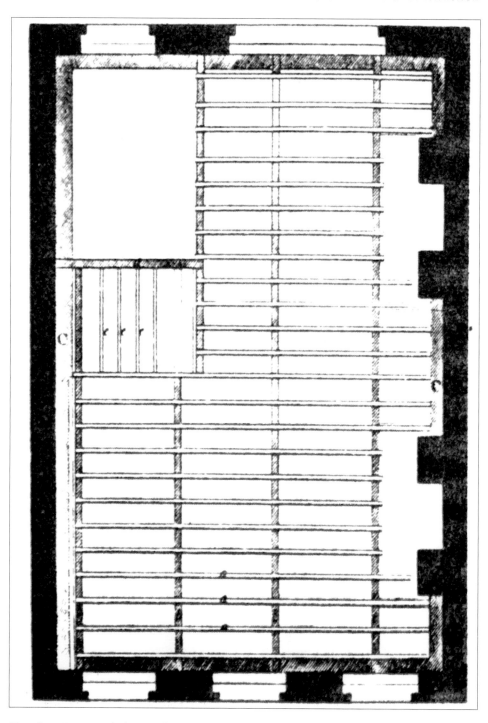

Plate from Peter Nicholson's *The New Practical Builder and Workman's Companion* of 1823. This offers detailed instructions on the choice, positioning and size of wooden joists to be used in the construction of floors.

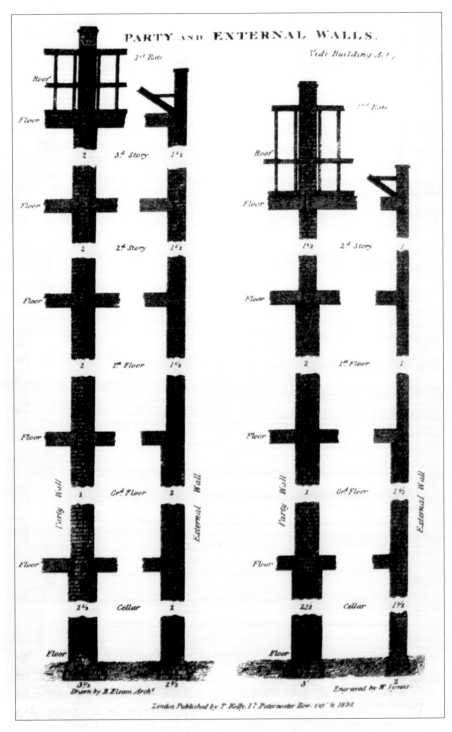

Nicholson's pattern book of 1823 also provided details for the selection, thicknesses and use of brickwork in the construction of 'party and external walls'.

4

LIFE AND SPACE

The Georgian terraced house was essentially built to cater for the needs of the aristocratic, mercantile and wealthy families who flocked to the new developments in the towns and cities across the British Isles. These households included the family members, as well as their serving staff. The former included the husband, wife and a number of children: usually two or three. The scale of the household staff depended on the resources of the residents. The more prosperous families, who occupied the larger houses, might have a cook, a maid and a manservant. They might also have a housekeeper and a governess. Modest families, in contrast, might have to make do with a single serving girl.

The internal functional arrangement of the house was divided into three broad divisions where the family's domestic and social life was lived out. These included the reception areas, the family areas and the staff areas – with each floor fulfilling a specific purpose. The ground and first floors acted as reception areas where the family lived and entertained their visitors. The second floor contained the bedrooms. This was the reserve of the family members, while the top or attic floor functioned as staff accommodation, with the occasional inclusion of a nursery for children. The basement was the reserve of the servants and this held the kitchen, a larder and staff accommodation. The overall result of this arrangement was a floor for cooking, a floor for eating, a floor for entertaining, a floor for sleeping, and a floor for the household servants. In reality though, these internal arrangements often varied in response to the domestic requirements of the individual owners. For example, the composer Handel used the first floor of his house in London for music and composing.

Whichever use was decided upon, the standard layout of one floor directly above the other exploited the narrow width of the house to the maximum, particularly where family living was concerned. The same layout, however, imposed heavy work duties on the staff. Deliveries were received in the basement. The family meals were prepared in the kitchen and had to be delivered up to the ground- or first-floor level, or higher up, following which the used dishes had to be returned to the kitchen for washing. The fires in the ground and upper floors had to be lit, fuelled and then cleaned out afterwards. Also, beds had to be made up, and laundry had to be collected and brought to the basement for washing and drying.

The houses contained no bathroom facilities, so vessels of hot water for washing had to be brought from the kitchen up to the bedrooms and these had to be returned to the basement afterwards. Also, the houses were provided with no sanitary facilities, so chamber pots were kept in the upper rooms for this purpose. These had to be collected, brought to the cess pit to be emptied, cleaned and then returned to the various rooms. The consequences of these household duties, along with a myriad of others, meant that the serving staff had to spend a great deal of time and energy making their way up and down the stairs between the various floors.

The same economic resources that limited the size of the house and the number of household staff also influenced the extent of the interior finishes. Initially though, the interiors of most Georgian terraced houses were sparse, with minimum furniture. The well-off families had the largest and most elaborately decorated houses, while the less wealthy families made do with whatever their individual circumstances allowed. In all cases, the degree of decoration matched the hierarchical nature of the floors, with the highest level of decoration concentrated on the ground- and first-floor levels. The level of decoration was restrained in the bedroom floor, almost eliminated in the top storey, and was non-existent in basement.

Before looking at the various floor levels in detail, it is necessary to pause and say a little about the most visible internal finish of the house: the plasterwork. It will be remembered that the structural walls of the house, that is, the front, back and party walls, were built with brick. The transverse wall, which separated the front and back rooms of the house, was also brick-built. Elsewhere the walling of the rooms took the form of stud partitions. These partitions were built with lengths of wooden framing, or studs, with the door frames set into them. The studs were than faced with thin wooden strips, or laths, laid across the studding. The plaster was then applied to the laths, keyed into the space between the laths and then finished smooth. The plaster itself was made from a mixture of sand, lime and water. The same process was followed in creating the plaster ceilings. Here the overhead wooden floor joists were sheeted with laths and than plastered over.

The plastering of the brick walling varied. In some cases the plaster was applied directly to the brickwork, while in other cases laths were applied to the brick face and then plastered over. Either way, the plaster was applied in three layers and then finished in a carefully applied final coat. At the point where the ceiling and wall met, the cornice was formed. Here the moulded shape was gradually built up with several layers of plaster. This was finally completed to the required outline by the application of a finishing coat.

Entrance Hall

The entrance hall, on the ground level, is the first room the visitor to the house experienced and every effort was made to create a favourable impression. Here the narrow passage at one side of the house provided access to the two main rooms and to the stairs that lay beyond. Initially the hall would have been dark, but the introduction of a fanlight over the door succeeded in providing a sufficient level of daylight to illuminate the hall. The floor was generally wooden, although floor tiling can be found in some larger houses. These tiles were usually marble or Portland stone and tended to be laid in regular geometric patterns. The tiling is carried on brick arches, or vaults, which can often be noted in the ceiling of the basement directly underneath.

Initially the plastered walls were limewashed or painted, often in pastel colours such as greys or greens. Another practice involved painting the walls to imitate stonework with its geometric pattern, smooth face and fine mortar lines. An outstanding example of this can be seen in the Georgian House Museum in Limerick. Here the original marbleised painted blocks cover the walls of the hall and the stairwell. At the top of the walls, a moulded cornice marked the junction between wall and the ceiling. This could have a simple pattern formed by the plasterer from standard lengths of plaster or wooden mouldings fixed to the walling. Alternatively, a complex hand-crafted cornice could be crafted by the plasterer where required. The plastered ceiling could be plain, although highly decorated ceilings with complex patterns can be found in larger houses. A centrepiece, or ceiling rose, helped to accentuate the centre of the ceiling. The rose, which often took a stylised floral form, was usually factory made and fixed to the underside of the ceiling, where it served a double purpose. It provided a point from which to hang an oil lamp and at the same time helped to disguise the heat marks from the lamp.

Stairs

Halfway along the entrance hall was an archway, which divided it from the stairwell beyond. This usually took the form of a semicircular decorated arch supported on each side by ordered rectangular pilasters built into the walls. The staircase was a particularly significant element in the Georgian terraced house and consisted of a sequence of wooden steps or threads that extended upwards to first- and second-floor levels, in a series of landings and half landings. The outer edge of the staircase, or string, followed the line of the steps and was faced on the outside by a decorated triangular panel. The uprights, or balusters, rose in pairs from the edge of the string. These were turned in a variety of shapes and carried a continuous moulded handrail. The balusters were generally painted and the hardwood handrail was polished. In the early period the corners of the handrail were marked with a heavy square post or newel, although this was soon disregarded.

The staircase stopped at the second-floor level where the balusters and handrail returned and died into the side wall, while at ground level the handrail generally terminated in a skilfully crafted spiral. Access from the second floor to the top or attic level was provided by a narrow set of service stairs tucked into one corner. Natural light to the stairs was provided by the tall, round-headed windows on the half landing that opened onto the back of the house. In the more modest houses the staircase could be less elaborate with a closed string. At the opposite end of the eighteenth-century social scale, a number of large houses were provided with stone staircases. In these cases the staircase had delicate metal balusters and handrails. Here the light moulded stone threads were cantilevered out from the side wall to give an almost floating impression.

Dining and Drawing Rooms

The ground- and first-floor areas of the house offer the most vibrant and attractive aspects of the Georgian terraced house, as they possess a range of common outstanding features. For this reason, it is worth considering both floors together. The dining room and the parlour take up the largest space on the ground floor and were usually elaborately decorated and furnished to impress visitors to the house. The parlour faces onto the street and seems to have acted as an occasional family room or library. The dining room, on the other hand, overlooks the rear garden, although it is worth noting that these uses were at times interchangeable. It all depended on the requirements of the individual occupiers. The dining room was used for entertaining guests and it was arranged with a large dining table set in the centre of the room, while an alcove in the dividing wall often held a serving table. The owner and his guests had their meal around the table, and when the meal was finished the dining chairs were moved to the sides of the room. At this point, the ladies withdrew to the drawing room on the first floor, or to the parlour in the next room in the case of the smaller houses.

As soon as the ladies left the dining room, the gentlemen took their seats around the walls to talk and drink. As there were no lavatories in the house and a large quantity of alcohol was generally consumed, the gentlemen relieved themselves into chamber pots. These were stored in small cabinets and placed in one corner for use, or could be passed around under the table. It must be assumed that the ladies in the drawing room followed a similar practice. In addition to the dining room and the parlour, the accommodation of the larger houses often included an annex at the rear. This could be used as a small family sitting room, a library, or a music room, and could be entered from the hall or directly from the dining room.

Characteristically, the ground- and first-floor rooms of the Georgian terraced house had six main features. These included the flooring, walling, doorways, windows, ceilings, and fireplaces. With the exception of the basement, and occasionally the hall, the flooring through the house was wooden. This consisted of wide wooden boards closely butted together. The floor boards were sometimes painted and were occasionally covered with rugs, with the flooring exposed around the edges. Wall-to-wall carpeting was extremely rare in the Georgian period.

In the early part of the eighteenth century the walls of the dining and drawing rooms were often panelled. The panels were fixed to the walls and the joints between the individual panels were hidden by raised moulding. By mid-century this panelling went out of fashion and the walls were plastered, although in some instances the lower section of panelling continued in use for some time. Where the panelling was completely dispensed with, a picture and dado rail were fixed to the wall.

Family paintings and landscape scenes highlighted the status of the occupier and these were hung from picture rails. These were lengths of wooden moulding that were placed just below the cornice level and extended around the walling. This was sometimes dispensed with and replaced by a slim, high-level brass bar on which the paintings could be hung. Lower down the wall, the moulded dado rail stretched around the sides of the rooms at chair height. This prevented the backs of the chairs from marking or damaging the wall plaster. Plasterwork by its nature is brittle, particularly at its edges, and in order to combat this, a moulded wooden skirting was fixed at floor level to protect the plasterwork where the wall met the floor.

Where panelling was not used, the decoration of the ground- and first-floor walls took several forms. The walls could be limewashed in a range of colours. Initially the colours were limited to pastel shades, but these soon gave way to brighter and richer colours. In exceptional cases, such as in 1 Royal Crescent in Bath, the paintwork was replaced by fabric hangings. The fabric was stretched over wooden panels, framed with narrow brass edges and fixed to the walls. This was a very expensive process and was superseded by wallpaper. This was also very expensive in the early part of the eighteenth century, but as costs gradually reduced, wallpapering became popular. In these cases, floral and geometric patterns were mostly favoured. Today, few instances of the original wallpaper remain intact. Fortunately, isolated scraps of original paper are known to have survived and this has allowed accurate copies to be reproduced and hung. In a number of instances, small pieces of original wallpaper have been framed and hung over the reproduced work.

Doors

Wooden panelled doors provided access to rooms on the ground- and first-floor levels. These were generally given six panels and were very often painted in shades of brown. On the second and top floor, where the rooms were less important, the number of panels was often reduced to five and four. The door and frame was always set into the partition and walls, where the joints between the frame and the walling was hidden by architraves. This was a flat wooden moulding that stretched around the top and jambs of the opening. In the more elaborate houses the number of panels might be increased to eight, and the tops of the architrave projected outwards in the form of shoulders, at the sides and base. In other cases, the head of the doorway might be crowned with a decorated panel or a triangular pediment. These served to emphasise the importance of the door. Most doors were made from softwood, although mahogany doors and elaborate architraves were often a feature of prosperous homes. Occasionally there was an interconnecting door between the dining room and the drawing room. This could have a double leaf with a number of panels in each leaf. A standard six-panel door generally provided access between the dining room and the rear annex. However, when the annex door opened off the half landing, the panels were often replaced with glass and an overhead semicircular fanlight was included. Whatever form the door took, the door furniture always included a brass knob and a cover, or escutcheon, to the keyhole.

Windows

Both the parlour and the dining room on the ground floor had two standard Georgian windows. Here, each of the opening sashes was divided into six glazed panes and each sash could be lowered or raised as required. In this way, ventilation to the rooms could be controlled by opening the top or bottom sash, or both. Each of the windows was framed on both sides by projecting boxes, which contained the shutters. These were splayed outwards from the face of the window, a feature that helped to reflect daylight into the rooms. When the boxes were closed, the shutters were hinged and folded so as to fit behind the splayed face, where they were hidden from view. When the shutters were required, the splayed panels were opened and the shutters swung across the window sashes. These shutters served a number of purposes. They offered a measure of security, but they were also used to keep the room warm and could be used as sunshades to protect the furnishing. In most cases the shutters were arranged on two levels, one above the other; so that the top or bottom part of the window could be blocked off as required. In addition, window seats were sometime slotted between the shutter cases at the base of the window. Curtains seem to have made a rare appearance, particularly in the early years of the eighteenth century, but as fabrics became more available elaborate curtains with wide swags and tails made an appearance and were secured from above the window.

Ceiling

The ceilings in the ground and first floor of most Georgian terraced houses have three components. These are the cornice, the main ceiling and the ceiling rose. The design of the cornice was dictated by the resources of the owner. As was the case with the hall, the cornice in the modest houses was made up of a simple geometric moulding, often made with wood and painted. This stretched around the room at the junction of the walls and ceiling. In the more well-off households, a more elaborate cornice was applied. This could include a selection of Renaissance elements such as mouldings, brackets, scrolls, dentals, and egg-and-dart motives. These could be purchased in lengths and fitted into place by the plasterer. In the more prestigious houses, the cornices could be handcrafted on site by the plasterer. In these cases a frieze was often added. This was a deep plaster band placed immediately underneath the cornice. It usually had a swag or similar pattern and followed the line of the cornice around the room.

Another feature of the larger houses was the decorated ceiling, which could be given elaborate geometric or stylised floral arrangements. The ceiling rose became a common feature of the dining and drawing rooms from the early nineteenth century onwards, as oil lamps became popular. Prior to this, light was provided by candles that could be moved around the house as required. Standard plaster ceiling roses could be purchased from manufactures but, as was the case with the cornice, very elaborate examples with geometric or stylised floral designs could be created by the plasterer in the houses of the well-off.

Fireplaces

The fireplace is perhaps the focal point of the dining and drawing rooms and consists of a decorated frame that surrounds and encloses the fire grate. During the early period, the fireplaces were positioned in the corners of the rooms, but later the fireplace was shifted to the centre of the party wall in each room. At this point, a section of the party wall was widened and projected into the room to form the chimney breast into which the fireplace was set. These chimney breasts were introduced on all floor levels and extended from the basement upwards through the attic to support the structure of the chimney overhead. This had the added effect of strengthening the structure of the party wall. The flues from the various fireplaces on each floor were gathered into the chimney breast and directed to the chimneys. The cast iron grates into which the fire was placed were set into the fireplace opening, from where the smoke was channelled into the flue. The early grates were essentially wide baskets and were particularly suited for burning logs. Later on, as coal became more available, the size of the basket was reduced to facilitate the burning of the coals. A further improvement to the fire grate was introduced when hob plates were attached to each side of the grate. These provided a small platform base where water could be heated from the sides of the fire.

The fireplace surrounds were a major decorative feature of the rooms and reflected the status of the household. Marble or stone was used in the houses of the wealthy, where the uprights and crosspieces were richly carved and decorated. Alternatively, wooden surrounds, often painted to imitate stone, were the norm in the more modest houses. However, the surface appearance of some fire surrounds can be deceptive, as it is not unusual to find elaborately carved wooden fire surrounds painted to imitate stone. How often the fires in the house were used is uncertain. Certainly the small size of the grates would not have been sufficient to heat the large rooms with their high ceilings. It may be that the fires on the ground and first floor were provided mostly for atmosphere and the fires in the bedrooms were lit only when the occupant was ill.

First Floor

The first floor held the drawing rooms and was the most important floor in the house. It was generally regarded as the 'piano nobile', the noble floor. The principal room was at the front and stretched across the full width of the house. It was well above the noise and clutter of the street level and it was where the family's major social functions were held. The back room acted as a smaller drawing room, and it was here that the ladies took their tea or chatted and played cards after leaving the men in the dining room below. This back room could also act as a small family room. As was the case with the ground floor, the drawing room walls could be panelled or painted. The first floor was also provided with the most elaborate skirting boards, cornices, ceiling roses, and fire surrounds – all emphasising the floor's importance.

The window and shutter arrangements followed that of the ground floor in style, although the spacing and heights varied. The front room, depending on its size, had two or three windows spaced across its width. These were the tallest in the house and the sashes were given fifteen panes. The use of panelled doors was similar to those of the ground floor, with elaborate architraves, overhead panels and pediments in the larger houses. In addition, wide double doors connected the front and back room together. Here the panelled door leafs could be swung back against the dividing wall to transfer the rooms into a single space for large social gatherings such as parties, dancing and singing.

The Second Floor

The second floor contained the principal bedrooms of the house and was generally reserved solely for family use. For this reason the applied level of finishes and decoration was less significant. The accommodation included a bedroom to the front and a bedroom to the back and perhaps a small dressing room attached to one of them. One bedroom was used by the man and the other by his wife, as during the eighteenth century it was common practice for married couples to sleep apart. The ceilings of the rooms were lower and this was reflected in the heights of the windows, which were given only twelve panes. The decoration of the rooms was more restrained and reflected the lower status of the bedroom floor. The skirting board was modest, the door panels could be reduced, the wooden floor was left bare except for a rug, and the walls were plastered and painted. A decorated cornice was included but it was less elaborate than that on the ground and first floors. The rooms were provided with fireplaces and surround, but again at a reduced level of finish.

The principal feature of the bedroom was the four poster bed. This was raised on high legs and had tall posts on each corner from which drapes were hung. These were draw across when the bed was in use to help retain heat, as the bedrooms could be very cold, particularly in winter. Later in the Georgian period, the full drapes were dispensed with, although the high corner posts and frill along the top were retained.

Other items of bedroom furniture might have included a small dressing table, a wash stand, and a wardrobe. The latter was equipped with a bank of drawers in which the occupant's clothes were kept folded, rather than the present practice of hanging. Where the occupant required a bath, a metal tub was set up beside the fire and was filled with hot water brought up in vessels from the kitchen. A chamber pot was also kept in the bedroom. This was often housed in a small cabinet, like a commode.

The formal part of the house ended at the second floor and to mark this, the ceiling of the stairwell was given a decorated cornice, ceiling and ceiling rose. At the same time the plan stairway to the upper or attic floor was squeezed between the front and back room.

The Top Floor

The top, or attic, floor contained the staff bedrooms and was divided into a number of small rooms, one of which doubled as a nursery when required. The rooms were partially set into the roof structure, and were provided with no cornices or ceiling decoration. The furniture was limited and included only beds and closets for the staff. This level might be upgraded to include children's facilities where a room was used as a nursery. The windows were the smallest in the house and had only six panes, often without shutters. At floor level the skirting was very basic and might have consisted of a simple wooden board. Similarly the fireplace, where it was provided at all, had a small grate and a modest wooden surround.

Basement

The basement was the service hub of the Georgian terraced house. The basement was reached from the hall by a narrow staircase, at the bottom of which was a series of wooden-sheeted doors, which provided access to the various rooms. The principal room in the basement was the kitchen, which stretched across the width of the house and looked onto the open area at the front, through which deliveries to the house were received. The cooking equipment, such as pots and pans, was kept in the kitchen, as were the cooking utensils. Meals and snacks were prepared and cooked here, water was heated and the laundry was dried and ironed. At the back of the basement were several small rooms including a larder, a scullery and perhaps a staff bedroom.

The kitchen was paved in plain stone slabs and the walls and ceiling were undecorated except for the painting. The principal equipment in the kitchen included a stout central table where the preparation and cleaning was carried out. Initially, the cooking was undertaken in a large open grate set into an alcove on one wall, but this soon replaced by a cast iron range. This incorporated an open fire, an oven, a hot plate and a water boiler to one side. The kitchen might also have had a dresser for the storage of pots and crockery.

The larder was generally an internal room where the atmosphere was kept dark and cool by the absence of a window. The walls were lined with shelving on which kitchen goods such as wine and candles were stored. The room occasionally featured a high-level shelf suspended by cables from the ceiling. This kept perishable goods such as meat, game and bread secure from vermin attack. A staff bedroom was often positioned at the rear of the house and faced the garden. This was sparsely decorated and equipped, and often acted as the housekeeper's bedroom. The scullery could be located towards the back of the basement, or under the entrance steps, and acted as the washing-up area of the house. It contained a stone sink and a water supply where the household pot washing, dish washing and laundry was done. The scullery might have been equipped with a hand pump for delivering water, where a service supply was available. Alternatively, the water had to be drawn by the pump from the well in the garden.

Above left: Behind the hallway, through an often decorated archway, the first flight of the stairway could be seen, while behind it the stairway to the basement was concealed from view.

Above right: In the early Georgian period, the lack of windows meant that the entrance was dark. Later, natural light to the hall was provided by the fanlight over the entrance door, and by narrow side lights where these were provided.

Previous page: The entrance hall was in effect the entry point to the Georgian house and was laid out to the highest standards to impress the visitor, with rich fixtures, decoration and fittings.

Above: Generally the hall had a wooden floor, but in the case of the more significant houses, geometrically cut and laid Portland stone or tiles were popular. In these cases, an arched or vaulted floor was inserted to carry the heavier weight of the stone or tiles, and to prevent cracking.

Right (both): The walls of the entrance hall were usually treated with a pastel-coloured lime wash. Occasionally walls could be stencilled to match foliage or painted to imitate ashlar with its fine mortar joints.

Above: The hallway to the Georgian museum in Limerick, for example, was painted to imitate rich-coloured marble blocks. Here the outstanding marbling effect was emphasised by the white-coloured doors and ceiling.

Left: The approach to the stairway of the typical Georgian terraced house is through the archway that separates it from the entrance hall. This can be a simple, high-level arch carried on brackets, or a formal arched opening with slim columns and a moulded plasterwork, through which the stairs can be seen.

Top: The cut-away model shows how plastering was achieved. First the wall and ceiling were lined with wooden laths. The plaster was then applied to the laths in layers and finished with a smooth surface layer. The cornice was similarly applied in layers and was finished to the required pattern with a hand-held moulded template. Today the use of plasterboard replaces the plaster-and-lath technique, and ready-made moulded cornice lengths can be purchased and nailed into position. However, the technique of plaster and lath is still widely practiced.

Middle: A plain moulded cornice at the junction of the walls and ceiling was a characteristic feature of the entrance hall in most houses. This could be applied with on-site plaster or with moulded and painted wooden lengths.

Bottom: In the case of larger houses the cornice could be very elaborate indeed, with hand-crafted Classical elements. Today, damaged cornices can be repaired by taking moulds from surviving lengths and re-casting the required profiles.

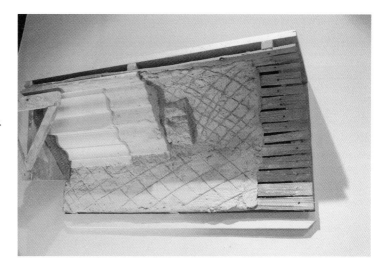

Above left: The hall ceilings of even the more modest houses were often executed in highly decorated plasterwork, often with intricate Classical or geometric patterns.

Above right: The artificial lighting of the hall was often provided by oil lamps, suspended from decorated ceiling roses. The heat from the lamps could stain the ceiling and this gave rise to the practice of suspending the lamps from the ceiling roses. This went some way to disguising the staining.

Above: Beyond the hall the main stairs provide access to the upper floors of the house. The wooden threads and risers were usually made from pine – or hardwood where the economic conditions allowed. The woodwork was always left bare, although today the surface of the threads can be worn after years of use. To conceal this and prevent slipping it is common practice to cover the stairs with carpet. This is often necessary, but a narrow carpet is best, to expose and express the original woodwork at the edges.

Right: The main staircase, which is positioned against the back wall of the Georgian house, provides access between the ground- and upper-floor levels of the house. This is achieved through a sequence of landings and half landings.

Opposite: The staircase is an important element in all Georgian houses as it winds its way upwards through the floor levels. Today many staircases are carpeted, although originally the wooden threads and rises were left bare.

Top: Generally the outer edge, or string, of the Georgian staircase was left open. Here the outside face of each step was marked by a decorated panel. This generally had a triangular form with a scroll or line-based decoration.

Above left: In the smaller houses, a solid rather than an open string was used and the uprights rose from the top of the closed string, although the hardwood handrail remained in use.

Above right: The open edge of the staircase is protected by a continuous balustrade that includes a pair of uprights on each step. The uprights were painted white or another light colour, along the top of which stretched the continuous mahogany, or other hardwood, handrail. The overall effect was one of lightness.

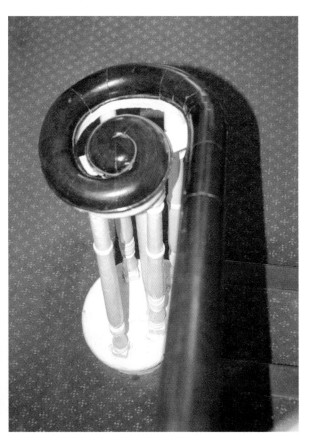

Above left: In the larger houses of the wealthy, the handrail at the end of the staircase in the hall was given a stylistic flourish. This involved twisting the end of the balustrade and the handrail in a flat spiral.

Above right: As the stairs were positioned against the back wall of the house, natural light could be supplied to the stairwell by means of half-landing windows. This is particularly so on the first landing, where a round-headed window not only supplied light, but offered an attractive feature visible from the hall.

Opposite top: In the early Georgian period the balustrade often included the heavy barley-sugar type of uprights, and square corner, or newel, posts where a flight changed direction. This, together with the woodwork, which was often painted brown to imitate mahogany, often created a dull atmosphere around the staircase.

Opposite bottom: The main staircase of the house only extended as far as the second floor, where it turned and terminated against the end wall. The reason for this was that the upper floor held the accommodation for the servants and that access to this level warranted only the plainest of stairs.

Top: In the homes of very wealthy families, stone replaced wood in the staircases. The stone steps were given open strings and they were projected out from the side walls of the stairwell.

Middle: The stone staircases were also provided with extreme, light, cast iron uprights and handrails. These could be either plain uprights, or have intricate Classical or naturalistic shapes, either way they reflected a high level of lightness and elegance.

Bottom: The individual steps in the stone staircases were delicately cut and shaped with moulded nosing, and could be given gently curved undersides. Structurally, the steps were built into and cantilevered out from the face of the wall.

Opposite top: The ground-floor dining room opened off the hallway near the stairs and faced into the rear garden. This is where the family had their meals with the food brought up from the kitchen in the basement below.

Opposite bottom: The dining room held the dining table and chairs, and these were placed around the edge of the room when not in use. The room was provided with a decorated ceiling, a cornice and fire place and many had a recess built into the walls to hold a serving table.

Top: The dining table and chairs were placed in the centre of the room when in use, and after meals, when the table was cleared off, the chairs were arranged around the edges of the room. However, as a rule, furniture in the Georgian houses tended to be sparse.

Middle: The parlour, in the front of the house, could act as a family room or as an office for the merchant who occupied the house. This room faced onto the street and visitors could be dealt with immediately on entering the house. Alternatively, the front room could act as a drawing room in smaller houses.

Bottom: In the larger houses an extra room, or annex, was included. This was entered from the first half landing on the stairs, and had a variety of uses, such as a breakfast room, library or music room.

Right: In earlier houses the walls of the various rooms were finished with wooden panels, although this practice seems to have gone out of fashion towards the middle of the eighteenth century.

Below: Where panelling was used, the panels were nailed to the wall and the joints were hidden by moulded framing that accentuated the panel work. The wooden panels were initially left plain or oiled, and later were painted in pastel colours.

Above: The walls of the Georgian houses were generally plastered and painted from the eighteenth century onwards. Earlier on, the plasterwork was given light blues, greens or other pastel colours. Only later in the nineteenth century did the brighter colours such as yellows and reds come into fashion.

Left: The idea of the panelling did not, however, completely die out, as wooden picture rails, dado rails and skirting boards remained in use. Also, low-level wall panels remained a feature of some houses.

Opposite above: The picture rail was fixed to the walls all round a room just below the cornice and, as the name suggests, family paintings and prints were hung from it. On occasions where picture rails were not included, a narrow, high-level brass rail was fixed to the wall and fulfilled a similar function.

Opposite below: The dado rail was a moulded strip of wood that stretched around the walls of the rooms at chair height. The object of this was to prevent the chair backs from damaging or marking the plasterwork behind.

Top: The wooden moulded skirting boards marked the point where the wall plaster or panelling met the flooring. The plasterwork at this point was very vulnerable to damage from chair and table legs, and skirting boards were used to protect the plaster.

Above: The skirting boards could be purchased in a variety of forms, ranging from having light profiles to elaborate ones. The skirting boards themselves were liable to suffer damage and scruff marks and were usually painted dark colours to disguise this.

Opposite: Wallpaper was a late feature of Georgian houses and did not come into general use until the late eighteenth century, when a range of designs including floral, animal and geometric images became available. In recent years it has proved possible to reproduce the original wallpaper of a Georgian house from surviving scraps. In a few instances a portion of original wallpaper has been displayed in a frame, and hung over the reproduced work.

Left: The important wooden, framed internal doors of most standard Georgian houses were made up of six panels framed with style, head, middle, and bottom rails. The panels are flat and are framed with projecting moulding. Generally the doors were made with fir and then painted.

Below left: In the doors of the less important houses or rooms, the number of panels could vary, but characteristically the flat panels lack a moulded frame.

Below right: Occasionally, important doors were given only four panels. In these cases, the significance of the doors was marked by the use of raised panels with moulded and bevelled edges.

Above left: All doors, whatever their status, were provided with an architrave. This was a side and top wooden section that covered the joints between the door frame and the wall plaster, the face of which could be plain or highly decorated.

Above right: The corner-shoulder of an architrave could be an intricate example of eighteenth-century woodworking, where the angle of the moulding followed a double turn.

Right: In the case of doors where it was felt that special emphasis was required, the architrave could be enhanced with small projections or 'shoulders' at the top of the door opening, and similar projections at the base.

Above: Another technique used to highlight the importance of a doorway was to crown the head of the architrave with a high-level moulding and a decorated frieze.

Left: In a number of more significant houses the importance of the doorway was emphasised by placing the door and architrave into a temple style portico. In one example this included shallow uprights, curved brackets, and a triangular pediment – the whole executed in wood and painted.

Above left: Mahogany or oak was generally used in the manufacture of the internal doors of the better houses. The number of panels might exceed six, or the panels might follow an individual arrangement. The wood was generally oiled to enhance the grain and so display the expensive wood to its best advantage. In addition, the doorway could be framed in an elaborate moulded architrave – often painted white.

Above right: A double door made an occasional appearance where it was required to connect the dining room and parlour in the standard house. Here each leaf was given three raised panels and a simple moulded architrave.

Above: All the internal doors of the standard house were provided with doorknobs, keyholes and escutcheons, as well as hinges – all usually brass.

Left: Glazed doors were rare in Georgian times and confined to special areas. This double door with its large glazed panels was positioned at a half landing, and in addition to serving a rear annex, it allowed natural light to enter the stairwell and hall below.

Right: The ground-floor windows usually have twelve glass panes; three across the width and four between the top and bottom. The proportion of the window panes are often held up as an example of fine proportion, but in reality the choice of the small panes was an economic decision: controlled by glass prices. Small panes of glass were considerabley cheaper than large panes in the Georgian period. Only when glass became cheaper in the nineteenth century did single-pane sashes became common.

Below left: Internally the Georgian windows were set between a pair of panelled shutter boxes. These housed the window shutters that could be swung open – partially or totally – to block the window for security or sunlight control. The up-and-down sliding movement of the sashes was controlled by cords and weights, with the latter housed and hidden in the sash boxes at the sides of the windows.

Below right: A window box was occasionally slotted in the space between the shutter boxes immediately below the window. This could be used for storage or as a discreet window seat.

Opposite: Many of today's Georgian houses have elaborate curtains with drapes and drops, although these only came into fashion during the late nineteenth century.

Top: All rooms in the Georgian house, with the exception of the basement, were given ceiling-level cornices. At its simplest, the cornice profile consisted of a shallow moulding. In the important ground- and first-floor levels the cornice was more elaborate, and incorporated Classical elements such as dental patterns.

Above: The cornices of the better-off houses were more elaborate, often with a range of Renaissance decorative elements such as ogee mouldings and alternating blocks, in addition to stylistic floral and egg-and-dart patterns.

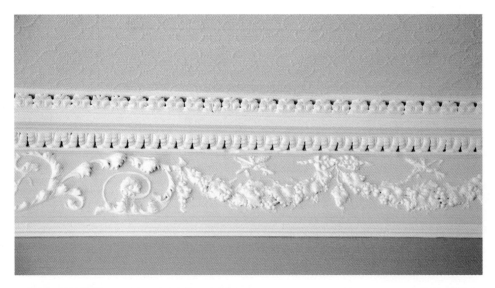

In the homes of the wealthy, the impact of the cornice could be accentuated by the addition of a frieze. This was a band that was placed immediately below the decorated cornice, so that the entire arrangement read as a Classical entablature. The frieze itself could be left plain or could include floral, swag or other Greek or Roman motives. A picture rail was often added immediately below.

Most standard Georgian houses had plain, white-coloured ceilings. An outstanding feature of the particularly large houses was the grand ceilings generally framed by elaborate cornices, with elegant geometric or floral patterns.

The plaster ceiling rose was a feature of many Georgian rooms and generally took the form of stylistic foliage arranged in a cluster and positioned in the centre of the ceiling.

Very complex ceilings roses could include an inner cluster set within a circle of stylistic garlands, from which a glass chandelier was suspended. The earlier chandeliers were lit by candles, but as oil became more available these were often replaced by small lamps.

Left: In the early Georgian homes, corner fireplaces were often built into the splayed angles of the cross walls between the front and back rooms. The grates were generally small and had plain, unassuming wooden surrounds.

Below: Initially, the cast iron fire grates were wide, particularly where only wooden firing was available. These had an open metal basket to facilitate the burning of large logs.

Above: As coal became more available from the middle of the eighteenth century the metal baskets of the grate were made narrower and were given brass stands. The narrow baskets concentrated the coal and encouraged it to burn more efficiently.

Right: Occasionally, flat hobs were included on each side of the grate basket. This allowed water or drinks to be heated from the sides of the fire.

Left: Fires were included in most rooms of the Georgian house and the fire grates were always set into fire surrounds. These consisted essentially of a pair of uprights and a crosspiece or mantle and could be made from wood or stone.

Below: In addition to the framing the fire grate, the surround acted as an important visual focus within the room. As well as providing heat, the fireplace and surround projected a sense of grandeur and hospitality.

Right: In the less important rooms of the house, the fireplace was utilitarian, with a small grate and a plain, undecorated surround.

Below: The material used in the fire surround could be deceptive. Stone or marble was used in the more decorative examples. In one example in Dublin, the rich carving had been painted over. When the paint was removed it was discovered the surround was made from wood. This was repainted, but a small section was left exposed to demonstrate the wooden manufacture.

The first floor of the house, or the 'piano nobile', held the drawing rooms and was considered the most significant in the Georgian house. This was where the family festivities

and social functions were celebrated. The walls could be colour-washed or wallpapered as wallpaper became more available in the late eighteenth century.

Above: The front drawing room was the largest and most important room in the houses. It extended across the full width of the floor and overlooked the street. Yet its first-floor position shielded it from the street noise and activity. It was given the richest doors, fireplace, cornice and ceiling. Like the dining room, the drawing room was sparsely furnished, initially at any rate.

Left: The back drawing room was used by the ladies when they retired after dinner, and was decorated and fitted out similarly to the front drawing room.

Both the front and rear drawing rooms have the most impressive skirting boards. These were elaborately moulded and could reach up to a foot in height.

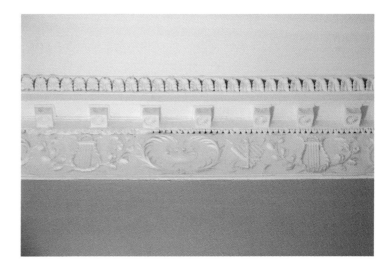

The importance and significance of the main drawing rooms was reflected in the elaborate cornices, which were often the most impressive in the house.

The drawing-room cornices, particularly in the drawing rooms of the wealthy, could be very elaborate indeed, with elaborate and delicate mouldings and friezes.

Decorated ceilings were a common feature of the drawing room, particular in the homes of the well off. These could include extended ceiling roses, as well as geometric and floral patterns.

The drawing rooms held the grandest fireplaces in the Georgian house. Marble uprights, crosspieces and mantle shelves were common even in the more modest houses.

In a number of instances the design of the fire surround was based on the Renaissance temple front, with half-round Doric columns, an entablature-like crosspiece and a wide mantle.

Above left: The drawing-room windows were the tallest in the house and often extended to fifteen panes, all framed by the projecting panelled shutter box.

Above right: Both drawing rooms were generally interconnected with double-panelled doors so that the two rooms could be extended into a single space, to cater for large family or social events.

Right: The built-in seating in the lower part of a window is an attractive and occasional feature of a room that allows the occupant to observe events in the street outside.

The second-floor rooms of the Georgian houses were used as bedrooms. They were set out with similar elements as the ground- and first-floor rooms, but with reduced levels of decoration and finish.

The owner and his wife commonly had separate bedrooms during the eighteenth century. The lady might have her own separate dressing room or the husband his.

Right: The bedroom skirting boards were not as elaborate as on the ground and first floors and were generally characterised by a shallow moulding.

Below: The bedroom cornices tended to be the plainest in the house. These had simple moulding and reflected the low status of the bedroom floor.

Left: The bedrooms were usually equipped with a small fireplace that seems to have been lit only when the occupants were unwell. The room furniture was sparse as usual and included little more than a bed and a wardrobe.

Below: The wide four-poster bed had tall legs and could sometimes be reached only by wooden steps. The bed was usually enclosed by full-length drapes that were pulled across to protect the occupant from the night cold.

Above: The washing arrangements in the bedrooms were usually a basin and water jug that could be incorporated into a wooden stand. Hot water, when required, was brought from the basement kitchen.

Right: The bedroom windows were lower than those of the drawing room, with twelve panes. This reflected the reduced height of the room. Here the shutter cases were simpler, with the single doors on each side and panelling at the lower level, all usually painted white.

Above: The main staircase of the house ended at the second-floor level. This was often reflected in the decoration of the stairwell ceiling, which included a decorated cornice and ceiling rose.

Left: The staircase from the second-floor level to the attic on the top floor was used by the household staff. It was considered unimportant and was squeezed into the narrow space between the front and back bedrooms, often without and balusters or handrails.

In the attic or top floor, bedrooms were essentially reserved for servants and were equipped with only a basic level of decoration.

Where the top floor took the form of an attic, it was slotted into the roof space with low, sloping ceilings and was divided into four small, cramped rooms, only some of which were provided with a fireplace.

In addition to staff accommodation, one of the attic rooms could, from time to time, be used as a nursery – a fact that reflected the social attitude of the period towards children.

Above: The attic or top floor had the smallest windows, with only six panes, and generally lacked shutters.

Left: The attic fireplace, in the rooms where it was provided, had a small grate set into a basic wooden fire surround.

 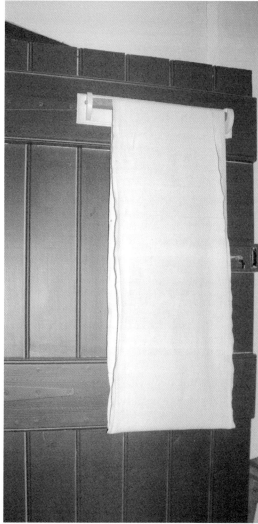

Above left: The basement was the workplace of the servants, and was reached from the hall by a plain staircase. These stairs were used only by the servants, and plain wooden uprights and handrail were considered sufficient.

Above right: The woodwork of kitchen doors was basic, and this was considered adequate for the kitchen staff. These had plain vertical sheeting held together with three cross rails, all painted in dark colours. In fact, the basement area was given no decoration whatsoever.

The kitchen stretched across the front basement floor. The windows and a doorway faced onto the open area at the front of the house, where deliveries could be made and staff entered the house.

The kitchen floor was generally paved with stone flags, or, on occasion, tiles. In the case of the former, the joints in the stonework would have made cleaning very difficult.

The food for the household was cleaned, prepared and cooked in the kitchen, before the staff had to deliver it to the family in the upper floors of the house. Afterwards, the remains and dishes had to be returned to the kitchen for cleaning.

The cooking equipment initially included an open grate, but this was gradually replaced by cast iron ranges towards the beginning of the nineteenth century. This was fitted into a wide opening in the chimney breast and included an oven, an open grate and a water boiler.

In addition to the range, the kitchen furniture included a large table, a dresser, shelving and perhaps a movable plate and food warmer.

In some Georgian houses, a staff bedroom was included in the basement accommodation. This was positioned at the back of the house and was generally occupied by the housekeeper. A small fireplace was provided, as was some basic bedroom furniture.

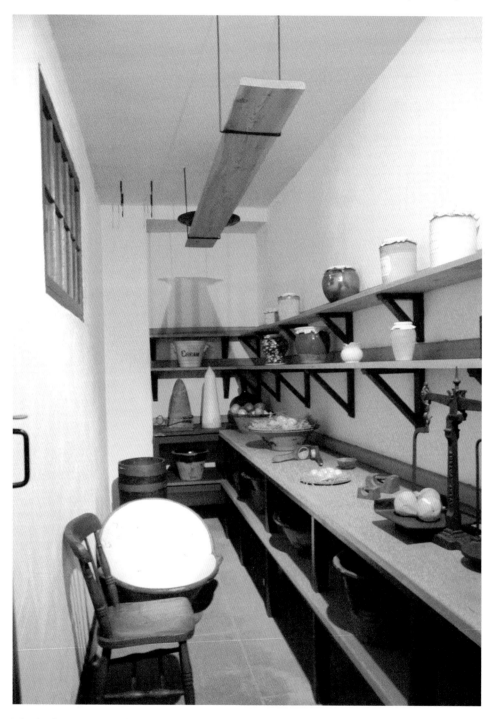

The larder was a small store that opened off the kitchen. This was lined with shelving and was used to store food and liquids. The room had no windows and every effort was made to keep it cool.

Above left: A scullery might be housed in a small annex at the back of the basement or slotted into the space underneath the entrance steps. This was equipped with a stone sink and possibly a water pump. Here the dirty kitchen utensils and the household laundry were washed.

Above right: Only where a local piped water supply existed was fresh water available to the Georgian houses. Where this was not the case, a well would be sunk in the rear garden. In either case, the water would be delivered by a hand pump that was positioned inside the house or close by in the garden.

5

THE GEORGIAN LEGACY

Legacy

During the first century BC the Roman architect Vitruvius highlighted the fact that good architecture is characterised by three ingredients: strength, commodity and delight. Strength refers to the structural stability of a building; commodity relates to the efficient use of space within the building, and delight to the satisfying environmental experience. Today, even the most modest of the surviving Georgian terraced houses embody these Vitruvian criteria, in a manner that is unquestionably excellent. In terms of technology, the brick, stone, wood, slate, and plaster used in the construction of the standard Georgian house were exploited to the maximum of their potential. Internally the houses were arranged in a disciplined system of vertical stacked spaces that allowed the efficient day-to-day running of eighteenth-century family life. Taken together, the length, width and heights of the ground- and first-floor rooms in particular present a spaciousness and proportional system that is both linked to Renaissance ideals and is eminently successful.

Externally, the brickwork, stonework, doorcases and windows combine to emphasise the vertically proportioned chequered house fronts, while the classically inspired internal elements, including the joinery, plasterwork, fireplaces, and staircases, contribute to the elegant spatial quality of the rooms. In summary, the Georgian town houses are outstanding examples of eighteenth-century optimism, urban art and craftsmanship, and reached a level of architectural accomplishment that has yet to be surpassed.

The emergence of the Regency style in the early part of the nineteenth century ushered in the close of the Georgian period. Grand, smooth stucco elevations with exaggerated classical elements replaced the texture of the uniform brickwork. Monumentality, with its full-height bay windows, rounded bays, porches, open arcades, and covered cast iron balconies, replaced the discipline of the brick chequer. Renaissance influences continued to impact on housebuilding activities for some time, particularly in the regional centres, but by the middle of the nineteenth century the Georgian era had passed, and few Georgian house proposals were entertained.

The dating of individual Georgian terraced houses can be problematic. Date stones can be a useful guide, but they may refer to refurbishment works, completed well after the initial construction of a house. Stylistic details, such as Queen Anne-style elements or exposed window boxes, can be taken only as an approximate guide, as there could be a considerable time lag between the London and the regional experiences. Documentary evidence such as deeds, maps and registers is more accurate, but again care must be exercised in interpretation.

It was the Victorians who ultimately brought the Georgian period to an end. Victorian society frowned on Georgian houses and considered their discipline and uniformity to be monotonous and dull. Domestic architecture moved on as landscaping and multi-coloured materials, as well as Gothic, Romanesque, Tudor and other historical references were all introduced.

Georgian Centres

It is fortunate indeed that so much of the Georgian fabric survives and remains in use across the British Isles, where four major centres in particular stand apart. These are London, Dublin, Bath and Edinburgh. The first two examples are essentially built with brick, while Bath and Edinburgh are stone-built: all of these offer a wide range of Georgian terraced town houses in their squares, crescents and streets. Outside of these major centres, smaller Georgian centres lie distributed all across the landscape. Some of these are comprehensive in scale, but most are modest Georgian quarters – amounting perhaps to a single square or a cluster of elegant streetscapes. In fact, so widespread is the survival rate of eighteenth-century developments, that it is a rare town indeed which cannot offer the visitor some examples of Georgian town housing. A complete list of these many centres is beyond the scope of this book for reasons of space, but a visit to any of the chosen centres scheduled below will not fail to delight.

One difficulty for those visiting the Georgian centres is the limited access to the interiors of the houses. This applies to most houses as they are held in private or commercial ownership and need to protect their privacy and security. Fortunately, a number of centres have Georgian house museums and these are also scheduled in the list of centres provided. It is necessary, though, to bear in mind that visiting hours to the museums vary. Some museums are open only during the summer months while others are closed for a particular day during the week. It is necessary, therefore, to verify the opening times before arranging a visit.

London

London is by far the largest Georgian centre in the British Isles. Together with its suburbs, such as Islington and Greenwich, it offers hundreds of squares and streets all lined with a rich variety of Georgian town houses. Special features include the vast range of brick houses that date from the seventeenth century onwards.

Museums

Denis Servers' House

18 Folgate Street, Spitalfields

Standard Georgian brick terraced house that dates from 1725 and has been restored and refurnished. The visitors are offered an atmospheric tour of the house, where the rooms are presented as if the occupants have just left.

Handel House Museum

25 Brook Street, Mayfair

Although dedicated to the composer Handel, the first and second floors of the house offer a good example of an early Georgian terraced house. The house itself dates from 1723 and originally comprised a basement, three upper floors and an attic. The ground floor was subsequently converted to retail use and the attic was converted to an extra floor. Today, the two floors offer panelled walls and typical eighteenth-century furniture.

Dr Johnson's House

17 Gough Square

Dr Johnson's House in the city dates from 1700 and offers an extensive collection of panelled rooms and eighteenth-century furniture.

Bath, Wiltshire

The city of Bath offers an astonishing range of stone-built Georgian town houses all carefully arranged in formal squares, impressive crescents, wide streets and a circus. Special features include the use of the local honey-coloured stonework.

Museums

No. 1 Royal Crescent

The large, stone-built, end-of-terrace house dates from 1767. It has been completely restored by the Bath Preservation Trust and offers visitors an extensive range of Georgian interiors and furniture

Chester, West Cheshire

Georgian Chester offers a range of interesting brick houses. Special features include the delightful Abbey Square.

Edinburgh

The stone Georgian houses in Edinburgh are laid out to an extensive and formal master plan in a series of squares, crescents and circuses. Special features include an extensive range of stone-built houses, often with the extensive use of elaborate Renaissance elements.

Museums

The Georgian House

7 Charlotte Square

The stone-built house dates from around 1796 and the basement, ground and first floor have been restored and are open to visitors. The various rooms include painted walls and eighteenth-century furniture.

Dublin

Georgian Dublin consists of six intact squares and streets filled with standard terraced houses and public buildings. Special features include the range of exceptional doorcases.

Museums

Number Twenty Nine

29 Lower Fitzwilliam Street

The brick-built, standard terraced house dates from 1790 and has been completely and sympathetically restored, offering a notable example of Georgian living spaces and furnishing.

Bristol

The Georgian sector of Bristol includes a formal square, wide crescent, Georgian streets and a range of brick and stone standard houses. Special features include a number of early Georgian houses.

Museums

The Georgian House Museum

Great George Street

The individual end-of-terrace house dates from 1790 and offers a range of eighteenth-century interiors and furniture.

Liverpool
The Georgian Quarter around Canning Street in Liverpool includes landscaped spaces with stone and brick houses. Special features include a wide range of distinctive doorcases.

Limerick, County Limerick
The Georgian sector of Limerick offers standard brick terraced houses laid out on an extensive formal street plan that includes a square and double crescent. Special features include the uniform Georgian streetscapes.

Museums
The Georgian House and Garden
No. 2 Pery Square
The standard brick terraced house dates from 1830. It is four storeys over basement, and has been completely restored. It offers an excellent example of Georgian interiors, furniture and a restored garden.

Whitehaven, Cumbria
The coastal town of Whitehaven has a range of standard houses laid out within a network of formal streets. Special features include the stucco-rendered houses.

Above: Georgian London includes a vast array of squares, streets and uniform blocks of standard brick terraced houses.

Below left: Date stones can be found on the wall of a house or at the end of a terraced block.

Below right: The Handel House Museum in London is confined to the first and second floor of 25 Brook Street. Here the floors have been restored with their Georgian interiors and furnishing.

Above: Georgian Bath has an outstanding range of delightfully attractive honey-coloured stone houses set in terraced blocks, as well as the streets, squares, crescents and circuses of the city.

Right: No. 1 Royal Crescent museum in Bath offers a large, excellently restored and furnished end-of-crescent house.

Georgian Edinburgh has a remarkable range of circuses, crescents and palace-fronted housing.

Above: Georgian Dublin has a range of Georgian squares with standard brick houses and elaborate doorcases.

Left: The Georgian House Museum in Edinburgh offers a partly restored and furnished mid-terrace house.

Right: Number Twenty Nine, the Georgian house museum in Dublin, is a standard terraced house, fully and sensitively restored and furnished.

Below: Bristol has a wide range of Georgian town houses and streets, as well as Queen Square and the Royal York Crescent.

Above: Georgian Limerick has a network of Georgian streets, squares and uniform housing blocks, all laid out to a uniform grid plan.

Left: The Georgian House Museum in Bristol is a restored stone-built merchant's home, with a range of Georgian interiors and furniture.

The Georgian House and Garden Museum in Limerick offers a fully and expertly restored, decorated and furnished standard brick terraced house and garden.

Also available from Amberley Publishing

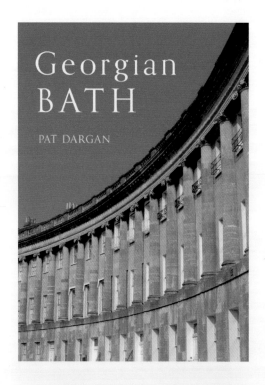

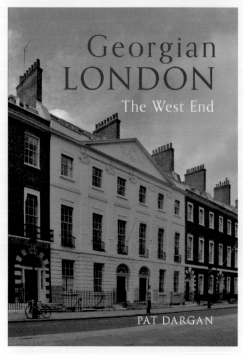

Available from all good bookshops or to order direct
Please call **01453-847-800**
www.amberleybooks.com